Good
For
Nothing

The Beauty of Islam and the
Ugliness of Muslims

A COLLECTION OF ARTICLES

Taj Siddiqui

Preface

In the name of God, the Most Gracious, the Most Merciful.

I am a practicing Muslim blessed with a bleeding heart. This book is a collection of short articles that I penned for local magazines during the last ten years. The theme of these articles can best be described by the quote from the famous Irish playwriter George Bernard Shaw. "Islam is the best religion and Muslims are the worst followers."

Quoting Prophet Muhammad (pbuh): "The People will soon summon one another to attack you in the same way as folks who are eating invite others to share their food." The Muslims of the twenty-first century have lost their dignity and have become the punching bag and laughingstock of the world.

This is my attempt to describe the beauty of Glorious Islam and the ugliness and stupidity of its followers. I am trying to peel off the sugar-coating and show the Muslims the oozing sores of their ugly practices and dangerous mindset, underneath the holy facade of their ritual prayers and religious traditions. Hopefully, they will stop rinsing the surface of the mirror and start cleaning their faces.

May God help us and guide us. Ameen.

Taj Siddiqui
Florida, USA
August 2022

Dedication

To my grandchildren, precious assets of my life

Sameer, Maya, Maryam, Sarah, Ali, Arman, Zainab and Zara

Hope and pray that Muslims of their
generation will be better than mine

Acknowledgments

My Sincere Thanks to

Sadrul Fasihi for his valuable guidance and advice

Josephine Shih Gordy for her detailed and comprehensive
work on editing and proof-reading

Rajeswari Bevara for her flawless job on
Designing and Formatting

A very special thanks to my wife, Meh Jabeen,
for her patience, understanding, and unmatched support

Contents

Good for Nothing

L ast week we were invited to our friend's home, Abdul and his wife, Katharine. We have known them for over 30 years. Our children grew up playing together. During dinner, their daughter Salma asked me, "Uncle, I want to marry a boy in my college. His name is Mike. My father tells me that I am not allowed to marry him because he is an infidel". Instead of answering her, I politely told her that it was too early for her to get married, and besides, there are many good Muslim boys in our community. She looked at me as if I had told her a big lie and left the dinner table in a bad mood. That night I came home very depressed and had horrible nightmares of running from infidels who were tightening their circle around me with their traps and long ropes.

The next morning I woke up late, not feeling good with an upset stomach. I rushed to the bathroom and sat on the toilet seat. I heard a voice saying, "No, no, you can't use me; I am the invention of an infidel." I looked around and saw nobody. The voice came again, in clear English. "I was designed and developed by infidels. Why are you benefiting from their findings, their inventions?" I said, "I have an upset stomach. Where do I go for relief?" The toilet replied, "This is not my problem. You should have thought about it years and years ago. You deserve to live back in the rural society where one can go out of the village, in the bushes, for relief. And while we are on this rosy subject, even the female sanitary napkins and baby diapers came from infidels." I got more depressed and ran out of the bathroom. Being depressed is my favorite activity. So, please don't start getting depressed with me.

The whole day went by like that. It was horrible and miserable. The indoor plumbing in the shower refused to operate. My cell phone was playing dead. The landline was also down, as the telephone was invented by an infidel. Mr. Computer changed my password and will not let me log in. The appliances: stove, refrigerator, microwave oven, washer, dryer, etc., refused to obey my commands. The air-conditioner won't let me touch the dial. My big screen TV, the surround-sound system, the blue-ray DVD player, nothing was working. And then my lights went off. There was no electricity in my house. We should have at least tried to convert Mr. Benjamin. My T-shirt and jeans started itching as I was wearing the dress code of infidels. In a panicky state, I ran out of my house to go to McDonald's. When I tried to start my car, it began to laugh at me. "Sir, the automobile was invented by an infidel. You guys should not have disposed of your camels and horses".

In this crazy state of mind, someone took me to the hospital. The doctor told me that the medicines were refusing to have any effect on my purified body as they were discovered by infidels. The apparatus and machines in the hospital were all invented by infidels. I asked him what my problem was. "Your problem, sir, is that you think you are the best, superior to the rest of humanity". Then I got mad at him. "What do you mean, of course, I am the best! I eat Halal food, offer Salat, pay Zakat, observe Fasting, recite the Quran daily, I did several Hajj, and perform Umrah every year. I did everything they advised me to do. What else do you want from me?" He said, "Sir, I have news for you. You may not go to Umrah anymore, as the airplane was invented by infidels".

I told the doctor to leave and started watching TV to divert my mind. The news was on. Over 190,000 Syrians were killed during the four-year-old crisis; Muslims are being killed by other Muslims; three million Muslims were displaced. Who are you, Yazidi, Alavi, Shia, Sunni? Let us get rid of you. How about the innocent small children in Peshawar. Who killed them? The infidels? No, no, this honor goes to the Muslims. At least this is one field where we left the infidels behind. The problem with the Muslim world is obvious, it is written all over the skies in bold letters. No unity and no leadership. No discipline and no organization. I started crying.

There are about 1.6 billion Muslims worldwide, and every fifth human being is a Muslim. Although the first-ever university in the world was founded in Morocco in the year 859 by a Muslim woman named Fatima today, there are no more than 600 universities in 57 Muslim countries. Not one

11

of these is in the top 100. The United States alone has close to 6,000 universities, 8 in the top 10. The literacy rate in the Christian world stands at nearly 90 percent, whereas in the Muslim world, it is close to 40 percent. Muslims spend 0.2 percent of GDP on research and development, while the Christian world spends 25 times more.

When we were busy building the Taj Mahal, they were establishing Harvard. The printing press was banned, and the printing of books did not begin in the Islamic world until the 19th century, four hundred years after it was established in the Christian world. The major discoveries by Muslims that have impacted modern civilization can be counted on our fingers. Muslims have received only 12 Nobel Prizes, compared to 170 awarded to Jews, mostly in economics, medicine, physics, chemistry, literature, and a few Nobel Peace Prizes. For every Jew, there are one hundred Muslims. I am getting more depressed.

That evening I came home, all beat-up, super-depressed, and sad. I knew I needed someone to lift my spirit; someone who knew who I am. I saw my wife cooking in the kitchen. So I rushed to her. "Oh beautiful, oh the princess of my dreams, oh the object of my love, oh the mother of my children, tell me how good I am". She looked at me with her fiery eyes, and I could clearly see the disappointment and hopelessness in her expression. She looked at this pathetic moron and checked me out from head to toe, and then in a firm and assertive voice, she very calmly said, "Good for Nothing."

Update

I wrote the original article about ten years ago. Muslims have since bottomed out and are now showing progress in science and technology. Recently two Muslim scientists have developed the vaccine for Covid-19. Their discovery has benefited the global population and is being prescribed worldwide under the banner of Pfizer.

From Bank Of America To
The Bank Al-Akhirah

How to take your wealth with you to your grave

A few months ago, I was inspired by an article penned by a Hindu writer. This is the story of a rich man who worked hard all his life and build a huge empire of wealth and honor. He has several businesses, properties, and other assets all over the globe. One of his wealthy life-long friends was very close to him. One summer afternoon they were on his expensive yacht, enjoying the vast ocean and clear sky above. Suddenly his friend started feeling chest pains, and then he collapsed. He was having a heart attack. They called for help and the friend was air-lifted to the nearest hospital. He expired in the air ambulance. Three days later he was standing in the cemetery looking at his friend being buried.

That night he realized that the end is coming, and he may be next. He saw his friend in the grave in a simple inexpensive white piece of cloth, alone by himself, empty-handed and with nothing else. He was not able to sleep. So, is this the end? He could no longer possess his wealth, his properties, his businesses, and everything that belonged to him. His huge empire of billions of dollars would stay here, but he could NOT take even a tiny portion of it with him. He panicked.

From the next day on he started asking his family, close friends, financial experts, spiritual gurus, and religious leaders to find a way to take at least some of his wealth to his grave. The unanimous answer was a plain and simple "NO! You have to leave everything here, and you cannot take a grain of rice with you." Suddenly the rich man started feeling very poor. He realized the real value of his empire. He became very depressed and went into seclusion. Very soon he was going to the grave with nothing, not a single dime from his enormous wealth worth billions of dollars. Then one day he found the answer.

Every day, on his way to his high-rise office building in his chauffeur-driven expensive car, he used to see a poor man selling toys and other cheap items on the sidewalk. The next morning, he stopped the car near that poor person, got out, and sat on the sidewalk next to him. Somebody offered him a chair, but he told them that he and the poor man were both of the same status. We both will go empty-handed. The poor man replied that this is not true. "You can take your wealth to your grave." The rich man jumped up in excitement.

He had been waiting for this answer since his friend died. He offered the poor man a hefty sum of money to tell him the way to accomplish this. The poor man told him to calm down and listen. "Have you read and understood our Nobel book the Quran?" The rich man replied, "no I have not. I did sometimes read it in Arabic, a language foreign to me. I never try to understand it. I have no idea what it tells us." The poor man replied, "it tells you how to take your wealth to your grave."

"When you visit a foreign country, you transfer some money to a bank in that country, so that you will have enough money to spend in the local currency when you arrive there. In the same way, you have to transfer your funds to the place where you are going." The rich man asked "I have my account in Bank of America. Where do I transfer the funds?" The poor man replied "it is called the Bank Al-Akhirah. You have to open an account in it and then transfer funds from Bank of America to Bank Al-Akhirah." The rich man said that he had never heard of this new bank. "Does it have any branch in this city?" The poor man replied, "it has branches all over the world, in every city, and on every street corner." The rich man was dying with joy. He insisted that the poor man take him right now to the nearest branch. He agreed and they both left.

They went into the poor neighborhood of the city. Narrow alleys with lots of potholes and trash everywhere. Walls were painted with gangster slogans and men sitting outside the houses drinking. A police car with a loud siren zipped by. They even heard a couple of gunshots in broad daylight. Finally, they stopped at a worn-down building with a small sign that was barely readable. It read like some kind of orphanage. The rich man was not pleased. "You promised to take me to Bank Al-Akhirah. This looks like an orphanage." The poor man told him that this was the Bank. "Go inside and open your account and make the first deposit." With some hesitation, they entered the building.

A man was dozing behind a desk in a small room. He woke up and greeted them. The rich businessman asked, "what the rate of return was?" The poor man replied "you will get it back seven times or more. If you deposit here $100 today, you will receive $700+ in your Bank Al-Akhirah account after you transit to the other life." The rich man again asked, "what kind of assurance? Who was promising this deal? Where was the written guarantee?" The poor man smiled and said that this transition of funds was backed and guaranteed by the one who created us. "He owns the universe, the earth, the skies, and everything between the two. My Lord is giving His Word to you mentioned and explained in the Quran, over and over, again and again." The rich man filled out the forms and signed up for the monthly contributions.

He went home with an unusual feeling of satisfaction, gratitude, and happiness. He had a peaceful and comfortable night and slept without any worries. The next morning, he created a charitable trust and started contributing to a long list of domestic and overseas charities. He informed his family about the transfer of funds and advised each of them to open their individual accounts in Bank Al-Akhirah. His wife asked him if he took care of the poor man financially. He said that the day was full of excitement and he completely forgot about it. The couple went back to the sidewalk to look for the poor man. He was not there. They searched for him for several days, but he was gone. He had accomplished his mission and was reassigned to a new project at a new location.

How Many More Muslim Women Have to Be Buried Alive to Get Our Attention?

A ssalamo Alaikum. Please pardon my frustration. I want to show you some ugly, open, and oozing sores of the Muslim world. Please pay attention, as these are our fellow Muslims.

Thousands of Muslim children and women are starving to death in Africa. They have to walk as long as 200 miles to reach an aid camp. A Muslim mother has to leave one of her children behind to die because she can carry only one or two children on these long walks.

In Pakistan, five innocent Muslim women were buried alive, and not a single person was found accountable. Their crime was refusing forced marriages and wanting to marry of their free will. No one was punished for this well-documented crime in 2008. In many other documented cases

Muslim women were gang-raped in broad daylight in the middle of the street, witnessed by several Muslim men, but nobody was made accountable.

In 2011, in Pakistan, at least 943 Muslim women were killed in the name of honor, of whom 93 were minors. Some victims were raped or gang-raped before being killed. Most of the women were killed by their brothers and husbands. During the same twelve-month period more than 8,500 acid attacks, forced marriages, and other forms of violence against women were reported in Pakistan.

In 2011, the great Islamic Republic of Pakistan secured the dubious distinction of being the world's number one global destination for searching the term 'sex' on Google, following its number one position in 2010. Also among the top ten are Saudi Arabia, Egypt, Iran, Malaysia, Indonesia, and other Muslim countries.

For Afghan women, fleeing domestic abuse, forced prostitution, or even being repeatedly stabbed with a screwdriver by an abusive husband, may land them in jail while their abusers walk free. Running away is considered a "moral crime" for women in Afghanistan, while some rape victims are also imprisoned because sex outside marriage - even when the woman is forced - is considered adultery. About 400 women and girls are being held in prison in Afghanistan for "moral crimes." They rarely find support from authorities under Afghanistan's "dysfunctional criminal justice system."

In March 2000, the Bangladeshi High Court ruled that prostitution as a livelihood is not illegal. Today, there are over 150,000 prostitutes in Bangladesh. It is a large sex industry, and hundreds of thousands of Bangladeshis visit sex workers every day. One such brothel, Daulatdia, services over 3,000 men a day and has more than sixteen hundred women living and working there.

For decades, Saudi Arabia was the only country that banned women from driving. This ban was lifted recently. This prohibition forced families to hire live-in drivers, and those women who cannot afford the $300 to $400 a month for a driver must rely on male relatives to drive them to work, school, shopping, or the doctor, even in cases of emergency.

Afghanistan, Nigeria, and Pakistan are the three Muslim countries where the human rights for Muslim women are the lowest in the entire world. How many more examples do you need ??? But we don't talk about these ugly and oozing open sores in Muslim countries, and our concerns are for the rights of Muslim women to wear headscarves and veils in non-Muslim countries.

In 2010, the Global Economy Journal published a comprehensive study, "How Islamic are the Islamic Countries?" It was co-authored by Professors Scheherazade Rehman and Hossein Askari, both from George Washington University, Washington, DC. Out of 208 rankings, New Zealand is on top of the list, Canada 7, the UK 8, Australia 9, Germany 17, France 18, and the USA 25.

Not a single Muslim country is in the top 37 places. The rankings of major Muslim countries are Malaysia 38, Turkey 103, Saudi Arabia 131, Indonesia 140, Pakistan 147, Bangla Desh 152, Egypt 153, Iran 163, Afghanistan 169, Syria 186, Libya 196, and Somalia 206.

In 2021 The World Justice Project released the rankings of 139 Judicial Systems in the world. Not a single Muslim country was listed among the top 30 places.

My brothers and sisters in Islam, this happens when a religion is decaying, and its followers are busy debating symbolic issues instead of confronting the real problems. We have lost our dignity and have become the punching bag and laughingstock for the rest of the world.

We have discovered the most convenient and comfortable escape route. We confine ourselves to the four walls of the Masjid, and we leave the rest of the planet outside the Masjid boundaries to Shaitan (devil). And Shaitan is dancing freely, laughing at us, and openly promoting all kinds of sins, from Shirk to Ribbaa (interest) and from pornography to Zina (adultery). Please, Mr. Shaitan, do not disturb our Salats and our Hafiz. Let us do the piety and taqwa inside the Masjid, and we will not bother you outside the Masjid.

When we go to Muslim countries, we go to their Masjids and Ijtemas (gatherings) of religious jamaats. We don't try to address the horrible crimes I have mentioned above, and we don't try to confront these issues. We don't ask Pakistani religious leaders why nobody stood up when five women were buried alive. We don't ask the Jamat in Bangladesh why they don't make prostitution illegal. We offer Salat with them, deliver speeches, and also try to help them with a few donations.

But have we done anything to help those ten and twelve-year-old girls selling themselves on the streets for only 50 cents in a Muslim country? They are our daughters, our sisters, and we should do our best to stop this inhuman business. How many more women have to be buried alive to get our attention?

Our Prophet (pbuh) was very clear in his message that he came to establish SOCIAL JUSTICE. This is what we need to be concerned about. WE NEED SOCIAL JUSTICE in Muslim countries, especially for Muslim women. Dignify the headscarf to the levels that non-Muslim women would like to wear as a symbol of prestige.

My sincere apology to many Muslims if I have offended you. I have self-censored a lot of material from this article. I am a Muslim, and I cry when I see this social injustice and horrible crimes without accountability all over the Muslim world. I am just showing you my tears. May God help us. Aameen.

Case Details Of Five Women Buried Alive (Copied)

August 10, 2008

The Asian Human Rights Commission (AHRC) has received information from a remote area of Baluchistan province of Pakistan, that five women were buried alive, allegedly by the younger brother of Mr. Sadiq Umrani, the provincial minister and a prominent leader of the Pakistan People's Party, the ruling party.

The Umrani tribe is mainly concentrated in the Jafarabad and Naseerabad districts of Baluchistan province which are about 300 kilometers from Quetta city, the provincial capital. In February 2008, Mr. Sadiq Umrani, the provincial minister for housing and construction, was elected to the Baluchistan Assembly.

According to the information received, five women were Ms. Fatima, wife of Umeed Ali Umrani, Jannat Bibi, wife of Qaiser Khan, Fauzia, daughter of Ata Mohammad Umrani, and two other girls, aged between 16 to 18 years. They were at the house of Mr. Chandio at Baba Kot village and to leave for a civil court at Usta Mohammad, district Jafarabad, so that three of the girls could marry the men of their choice. Their decision to have marriage in court was the result of several days of discussions with the elders of the tribe who refused them permission to marry.

As the news of their plans leaked out, Mr. Abdul Sattar Umrani, a brother of the minister, came with more than six persons and abducted them at gun points. They were taken in a Land Cruiser jeep, bearing a registration number plate of the Baluchistan government, to another remote area, Nau Abadi, in the vicinity of Baba Kot. After reaching the deserted area of Nau Abadi, Abdul Sattar Umrani and his six companions took the three younger women out of the jeep and beat them before allegedly opening fire with their guns. The girls were seriously injured but were still alive at that moment. Sattar Umrani and his accomplices hurled them into a wide ditch and covered them with earth and stones.

The two older women were an aunt of Fauzia and the other, the mother of one minor. When they protested and tried to stop the burial of the minors that were plainly alive, the attackers were so angry that they also pushed them into the ditch and buried them all alive. After completing the burial, they fired several shots into the air so that no one would come close.

The Significance of Ramadan

Why Do Muslims Observe Fasting

R amadan is the Muslim holy month, and fasting is obligatory. I want to take a commonsense approach to show
why fasting has been prescribed and what is the significance
of Ramadan. My goal is to reach citizens of all faiths. I am
not a religious authority, and please pardon any unintentional error. The intent is to give you only a simplified version of this topic.

Body And Soul

Islamic teachings guide us to two phases of our life: the first
focuses on this planet and the other after our physical death.
There are two worlds, the finite world we have on this globe,
and the eternal world of the hereafter, up in the heavens.
This finite world is regulated by physical laws, whereas the
Divine Laws govern the afterlife. We have an explosion of

knowledge about this world, but minimal knowledge about the hereafter world, only what is given to us by the Divine books and from God's Messengers.

We are human beings, and our existence consists of two major components the body and the soul. The body is created on this planet from elements taken from the earth. It is finite. It decays with time and eventually ends at death when it rejoins the earth. It is dirty and requires a lifetime of cleaning and maintenance. It is fragile and is targeted by various diseases. The human body has resulted from the act of sexual intercourse, so filthy that it is conducted behind closed doors and so dirty that we do not mention this act in a civilized gathering. Our body is a product of this planet, it starts here, and it ends here.

The second component of our existence is our soul, the *Rooh*. It comes from God and is united with the developing fetus in the mother's womb to shape and complete the structure of a human being. The soul is pure, clean, and innocent. After the body's death, the soul is taken back to God. The real me is the soul, and my body is just a vehicle provided to me to travel through life on this planet. Consider the program you are watching on the TV set. The real I is the program beamed from the satellite to the TV set, and the TV set is just the vehicle to deliver it.

The Objective Of Ramadan

Humans need to maintain their bodies as well as nurture their souls. However, our 24/7 schedule is built around the needs and desires of the body, and we hardly pay attention to our souls. The essential purpose of religious activities in Islam, and many other religions, is to control the desires of the body and to provide nurture to the soul. Ramadan is such an activity. In today's fast-moving lifestyle, we are flowing with the rest of the world and neglect the balance required between our body and our soul. The deviation from the right path starts unnoticed, keeps growing, and takes us in the direction of self-destruction. Once a year, Ramadan gives us the opportunity to check ourselves, where we are, and where we are heading. It gives us a chance to correct ourselves and steer towards the right track that cares for both the body and the soul.

Another objective is to awaken our thankfulness and appreciation for God. We get so occupied in our routines and daily rituals of life that we take for granted the many great rewards and blessings that are provided by God for our survival and livelihood. This is human nature, we do not appreciate daylight unless we face the darkness of night. With the temporary absence of food and other pleasures, we face reality and become more thankful to God when we break the fast. In addition, we also realize the agony of those less fortunate who are unable to attain these necessities and privileges of life.

Training Exercise

Fasting is obligatory for all adult Muslims when they reach puberty. Those who are sick, pregnant, elderly, or traveling may make up for the missed fasts later in the year. Ramadan provides us with an excellent month-long training exercise to practice self-restraint. It requires the total commitment of our body and our soul, round the clock. During this period, our schedules are focused on the needs of our souls more than the desires of our bodies. The daily routine of over 1.5 billion Muslims is adapted to achieve piety and obedience to God. This rigorous training in Ramadan is designed:

- To control and regulate our need for food and drink.

  (Absolutely no food, drink, or any other intake is allowed from dawn to dust, for approximately 15 hours)

- To control and regulate our need for sleep and rest.

- To control and regulate our desire for sex and evade lust.

  (Sexual activity is prohibited during fasting hours)

- To manage our emotions and temptations.

- To take charge of the actions and activities of our daily life, what we think, what we read & write, what we say, what we listen to, what we see, what we show, where we go, and whom we associate with.

- To elevate our thanks and prayers to God. In addition to the regular five times of obligatory prayers, offer *Tahajjud* prayers in the wee hours of the night or offer *Taraweeh* prayers with the congregation

- If workable, reside the last ten days and nights inside the mosque with complete devotion to God and perform all-night prayers on the Night-of-Power, one of the final ten nights of Ramadan.

- To read, listen to, understand, and seek to implement the Quran in our daily lives. (The Quran was revealed to Muslims during Ramadan)

- To volunteer for the charity, pay obligatory *Zakat* (2.5% of assets) to the underprivileged and offer food to the needy.

- To forgive others and to seek forgiveness from others.

- To amplify the performance of good deeds and gracious activities to fellow Muslims.

- To pursue righteousness and to obey God.

Health Benefits

Cleansing our bodies is considered to be an important health benefit of fasting. The body turns to its fat reserves for energy when food no longer reaches it. This process eliminates and neutralizes the toxins through various organs of our body. In addition, our digestive system is not in use during the fasting period. The energy that is usually being consumed there can now be used to improve metabolism and the immune system. Fasting also provides a break in the cycle of rigid habits. I personally quit my strong addiction to cigarette smoking during the month of Ramadan. However, the best outcome of fasting is the rejuvenation of our body and soul. You are at peace with yourself. You are doing good for yourself. The experience of pleasure, happiness, tranquility, and purity at the time of breaking the fast is unattainable from any other activity. The only way for a non-Muslim to enjoy it is to spend 24 hours with a Muslim family and fast with them.

Eid Celebration

Following the successful completion of Ramadan, Muslims celebrate the graduation of this month-long rigorous training and exercise in the form of a day of joy, happiness, and thankfulness. They offer thanks to God and pray for peace on earth and the well-being of fellow Muslims. Our loved ones who have passed away are remembered in our prayers. The day starts with the Morning Prayer in congregation along with charity and is spent visiting family and friends. Gifts, hugs, laughter, and delicious food are shared. Wear new clothes and perfumes by those who can afford them. Muslim children love the festivity and enjoy the gifts and the amusements.

I will conclude with my humble prayer to God. All praises and thanks to *Allah*. Oh *Allah*, please help us and guide us to diminish the sufferings of our fellow human beings and to care for and to provide support for them. Oh *Allah*, grant us good in this world and the world hereafter, *Aameen*.

Eid in a Syrian Refugee Camp

The material in this article was put together
from various sources on the internet.

My name is Eman, and I am 13. My brother Yousef is only two years old. Many months ago, we fled the civil war in Syria and now live in a Refugee Camp. It is a shame to call this "living." I lost track of time and places. However, I know that Eid is coming. Eid was a very happy day when we were living in Syria. In peace. My mother just told me that I will get married after Eid. At only 13. A joyous Eid and a joyful wedding. But there is a thick veil of sadness and sorrow on all our faces. Yousef doesn't care. He was born into terror, sleeping during shellings and shootings. Since we left Syria, we never heard from our father.

I do remember our last Eid in Syria. We had a big house in a nice middle-class neighborhood. I had beautiful clothes and all the luxuries of a comfortable home. Then the shellings and the shootings started. The planes began dropping bombs not too far from our house. One night, the soldiers came to our house and started flirting with me. I ran screaming to my mom. The soldiers promised to return. The next day, my father packed me, Yousef, and my mom into a car full of other strangers. At the border with Lebanon, we joined one of the many caravans that were being smuggled across the border.

I don't go to the bathroom at night. The so-called bathrooms are pitch dark, and predators hide waiting for us. Rats and snakes also crawl inside our make-shift tent. An abandoned shelter for sheep and goats has become our home. We met a man who promised us better living conditions. My mom, Yousef, and I, with many other girls, were taken to a house in the city, far from our camp. We knew that something was wrong. Men came out of that house and took selected girls with them. We were horrified and somehow managed to escape. I believe that the presence of an infant was not attractive to them. Yousef saved us. After this incident, my mom decided to get me married ASAP. It was for my own protection.

This is my friend Nidal. He is six years old. He fled Syria because of ongoing shellings, explosions, and shootings. He was playing in the street with friends when they chased him and started shooting. He saw men with guns taking his father away, who was then killed in the street. Nidal described the scene for us, "The planes were dropping bombs all around, and houses were hit with loud explosions. They were also hitting schools, and many children died. Men were running and shooting. What do I remember? People were being hurt. People were dying in front of my eyes. We should stop these shellings. Explosions lead to destruction, and shells injure people and kill people. The only effect is destruction, death, and wounded people. My home has been destroyed. We were in it when it was hit and fell. I feel as though all of Syria has been destroyed."

Nidal is showing us his new "home" in the refugee camp. This back end of a junkyard, a garbage-strewn dump, looks safe compared with the war back home that has destroyed the houses of the refugees and killed their families. So they have settled here. They have slapped together ten crude tents from scrap wood and plastic, including discarded billboard ads. Off in one corner is a hand-dug latrine, just an open pit surrounded by a piece of blue plastic sheet flapping in the wind. Everyone uses it. Imagine the filthy, toxic mess all around you. Feel it on your skin. Imagine eating here. The center of activity is a black plastic hose that comes out of the ground, connected to a spigot. It is the only source of water here. They don't know where it comes from, but they drink it, they bathe in it, and they cook with it. The kids have diarrhea most of the time.

Children play everywhere. Most of them are filthy. Virtually everyone has cuts or scabs on their fingers and toes. Snow will be coming soon, and nobody here has warm clothes or boots. Nidal, with another 11-year-old boy, comes to a pretty park nearby each day. They carry black plastic bags filled with packs of tissues and walk all afternoon along the winding paths peddling them to everyone strolling by. They accept whatever price people give. Each makes about $25 per month. This is the way they help their families.

Eid is coming, and yes, to be followed by my wedding. In the camp, there is no water, no sanitation, and no electricity. My friend Um Ahmed died in September. After three days of heavy rain, there was dirty, polluted, ankle-deep standing water everywhere. Um Ahmed started vomiting and was suffering from severe diarrhea. There was no medical treatment. She will not be with me this Eid. Yousef is developing jaundice, and it is getting worse. I hope he will make it to my wedding.

For over three years, the children of Syria have witnessed and experienced one horror after another. They have suffered indiscriminate violence and witnessed unspeakable abuse. Millions have lost loved ones, schools, and homes. Now in its fourth year, the war in Syria has killed more than 190,000 people and driven nearly ten million from their homes. And there is no solution in sight. There is a lack of humanity with respect to Syria because when we talk about Syria, we talk about figures. Nobody understands that kids cannot go to school on a normal day. The shelters in the Refugee Camps are not equipped for the freezing temperatures in winter. People lack water, sanitation, electricity, and medical help.

What have we done to deserve this? Oh Allah, where are you? Oh Allah, please help us. Please help us. Eid is coming, and I will be a bride after Eid. I want Yousef to be there with me. To celebrate Eid and to celebrate his sister's wedding. Oh Allah, please help these innocent believers. They are a part of the Ummah of your beloved Prophet. Peace be upon him. Aameen.

An Epic Love Story

Prophet Muhammad pbuh
and Hazrat Khadijah

Information and material adapted
from several sources on the internet

She was an ideal wife; theirs was a true love story. Love comes when you are not looking. She fell in love with him and, through a friend, asked him to marry her. He said yes. Their marriage was monogamous until her death 25 years later. Muhammad (pbuh) had no other wives while she was alive and had no children by any of his later wives. She was the first Muslim on this planet.

Loving Muhammad (pbuh) was the greatest thing that had ever happened to Khadijah, and he felt the same way about her. In a partnership of minds and hearts, Khadijah and Muhammad (pbuh) embodied what it meant to transform love into action and for those actions to have the power to change the world. They supported each other in what was important to them, and they actively encouraged each other to seek out and do what was right. Together, they were the best version of themselves, not just towards each other but to all those around them.

The marriage of Muhammad (pbuh) and Khadijah was most successful. It was blessed with felicity unlimited for both husband and wife. Khadijah dedicated her life to the service of her husband and of Islam. She spent all her vast wealth on strengthening Islam and on the welfare of Muslims.

Khadijah was a woman of beauty, intelligence, and superior character. She was highly sought after by the greatest men of Quraysh. She was married twice and had children with both her husbands. After her second experience as a widow, she chose to focus her efforts on her business instead of marriage, or so she planned anyway.

Khadijah was born to a father who was a successful merchant in their Quraysh tribe of Mecca. She inherited her father's skills at a time in history when society was male-dominated and dangerous. Upon her father's death, she took over the business and traded goods through the primary commerce centers at that time — from Mecca to Syria and to Yemen — hiring the most trustworthy men of character to brave the dangerous trade routes. Khadijah learned of the stellar character of Muhammad (pbuh), as well as his experience in managing caravans on the trade routes accompanying his uncle, Abu Talib. She hired him into her conglomerate and sent him with a trading caravan to Syria, accompanied by her slave, Maysara.

When the caravan returned, Maysara told her even more about the Prophet and his success in trading. Khadijah was then deeply moved and impressed and really wanted to propose to him, but she did not know how to express her thoughts to him. So, she sent one of her close friends, Nafisah bint Manbah, to the Prophet (pbuh). Nafisah asked the Prophet (pbuh) if she could inquire about a personal matter. The Prophet (pbuh) did not object. So, she asked him why he had been unmarried till now. He told her that he did not have financial resources. So, she asked, if he would be willing to marry a beautiful lady from a wealthy noble family and wealth who is inclined to marry him. He asked whom she was referring to. When she told him, he said he would be willing to marry her.

Muhammad's (pbuh) prophethood began during the 15th year of their marriage. His entire body trembling with the weight of Divine Revelation, Prophet Muhammad (pbuh) sought sanctuary in the arms of his beloved. He called out to Khadijah to cover him up and desperately told her what had just transpired. Khadijah wrapped him in a cloak and held him until his shaking ceased.

Khadijah was supportive of Muhammad's (pbuh) prophetic mission, always helping him in his work, proclaiming his message, and belittling any opposition to his prophecies. It was her encouragement that helped Muhammad (pbuh) believe in his mission and spread Islam. Khadijah also invested her wealth in the mission. When the aristocrats of Quraysh harassed the Muslims, she used her money to ransom slaves and feed the community.

To her husband, to her daughters, to the Muslims around her, Khadijah provided ceaseless love and support. Her steadfastness in the face of adversity was both inspiration and comfort, a sign that one did not need to be the Prophet of Allah in order to exhibit such power of faith. Indeed, to the one who *was* the Messenger of Allah (pbuh), she was the source of constant reassurance and love.

"Every day, Khadijah revived his spirits and restored his morale. Her cheerfulness cushioned him from the devastating pressures of external events, and he was able to face his enemies again with new confidence. The only happiness that he ever found in those years of horror and terror was when he was with Khadija. Sorrows and tribulations came in waves, one after another, threatening to overwhelm him, but she was always there to rebuild his courage and resolution in overcoming them."

Hazrat Khadijah died in 619, a few years before the migration to Medina. Though the Messenger (pbuh) understood that every human being belongs to their Creator alone, he was still plunged into sorrow. He lost the woman who had, for twenty-five years, been the love of his life, the intellectual match to his sharp mind, the spiritual counterpart to his heart full of faith, the one whom he held and who held him in return, and the mother of his children. The love of Prophet Muhammad (pbuh) and Khadija was immortal. When Khadijah died, Muhammad's (pbuh) love for her not only outlived her but actually went on growing even after her death. The year of her death was forever known from then on as the Year of Grief.

Hazrat Khadijah Shattered the Glass Ceiling 1400 Years Ago.

- The bride was older than the groom, she was 40, and he was 25.

- The bride fell in love with him, and she proposed to the groom.

- The bride was a widow and was already married twice before.

- The bride had children from previous marriages, and they now became part of the new family.

- They had a monogamous relationship for 25 years till death did them apart, in a time and culture when men used to have multiple wives.

- The husband and wife loved and cared for each other with passion and devotion.

- They treated and served each other at equal status, and the man did not pretend to be superior.

- The bride was a prominent and established business-woman. She was the employer, and the groom was working for her.

- The wife was a part of managing the household expenses.

- He was the last Prophet (pbuh), and she was the first Muslim human being on the planet.

- It is NOT the sunnah (practice) of our beloved Prophet (pbuh) to marry again with other women while his first wife was still alive and well.

The King and the Priest

There was a King, the god-king. He had huge palaces with an army of servants and lush gardens spread over several miles, a haram full of beautiful women, and a mighty superior army with no match. He ruled the country with pride and ego, with a fist of terror and evil. The people in his country were impoverished and dissolute. They were living in an environment of poverty, terror, and injustice. Eventually, people started dying of hunger and reached the point that they turned to eating rats.

And one day, they said enough was enough and went to the palace to see the King. They formed a large procession and shouted, screamed, and demanded food. The King didn't meet them because he didn't want to face them. His soldiers started beating the protesters and dispersing the crowd. But the King knew that they would return. Now that the revolution had begun, how long could keep them under his thumb? He was sitting in his garden, worried, and had no idea how to deal with this crisis. That was when his Chief Priest walked in.

The King explained the situation to the Priest and asked for his suggestion. The Priest started laughing and told the King to relax. He said, "Don't worry at all. I will handle it myself. You don't have to even talk to them." The King was delighted. The next day, the King and the Priest invited the crowd to gather in the Palace compound. This time the group was even more extensive and was more upset. The Priest appeared on the balcony to address the crowd. When the people saw the "heavenly" face of the Priest, they stopped shouting and became very respectful. They explained to the Priest that they were hungry and had nothing to eat, their children had no milk, and they were all drinking the same water into which they disposed of their wastes. "Please help us, please help us."

The Priest told them to have patience and not to lose hope. He explained that they were asking someone to help them, who himself needed help. The King was not the sustainer; God is the sustainer. When the King needs help, he bows to God and asks Him for guidance. When the King needs food, he prays to God for food. The King was himself a receiver, and the almighty God is the one and only giver. God is our sustainer, and He always will take care of us. We are all His children, and God loves us. Please pray to the almighty God to give you food and all the help you need. He has promised to listen to you and me. God is great.

The crowd started dispersing and planning to pray in large congregations. The Priest offered to provide local priests to organize and lead their communities. However, some folks were not happy and had more complaints. They told the Priest that the King's soldiers take their live stocks, destroy their homes and kidnap their daughters. "There is no justice, and no one listens to us."

The Priest told them again to have patience and not to lose hope. He told them, "You will be rewarded per your deeds, and you will be rewarded for what you have done. He is watching each and every one of us. This challenging time is a test for you from God. If you succeed in the test, you will be rewarded with a place in heaven in the hereafter. This is a very short life, a few years. Life in the hereafter is eternal. Just take the hunger and the cruelty and the injustice with a smile. Do not complain. Your destiny will be a higher place in heaven." Now people had a clear answer and left the palace compound peacefully. They were still hungry and were collapsing on their way back due to starvation and sickness.

After a while, the people of this country realized that the King and the Priest were playing a game with them, how they distorted their religion and the name of God to promote their self-rule. So, one day they again marched to the palace, armed with sticks and stones. Waves and waves of poor and hungry citizens destroyed the royal gardens and ransacked the palaces. They pulled the King and the Royals into the streets and butchered them. They unlocked the warehouses full of food and distributed it to the needy public. They took over the government and established democracy for the people and by the people. The Chief Priest escaped and was hiding in the elegant and great church that the King built for him.

The people did not kill the Priest as they still respected him. For them, he was the "face" of God. However, they confined him to the four walls of the church and told him that he had absolutely no authority outside the church from this day onwards. "We will commit all kinds of sins right under your watch, but you cannot stop us. We will declare gay marriage, abortion, adultery, and nudity as acceptable routines and norms of our society, and you cannot raise a finger to criticize us. You can preach inside these walls, but you cannot interfere with our daily lives outside the church. You will have no participation in our government or our laws. We are declaring the separation of Church and State."

The country started progressing, and the citizens became prosperous. They established tolerance, social justice, freedom of speech, and human rights. Institutions were developed, and higher education and the welfare system for the needy were promoted. They were following all the steps that their religion had initially taught them. They opted to follow scientific reasoning instead of religious faith. They achieved inventions that made outstanding contributions to society and the life of an ordinary man.

Many countries try to copy them. However, very few succeeded. Today most countries are still ruled by the "King" and the "Priest." Today, yes, today, hunger kills more people each year than AIDS, malaria, and tuberculosis combined. Every 10 seconds, a child dies from hunger. And they are still telling us not to complain. Be patient. You will be rewarded with a higher place in heaven. They are still using our religion and distorting God's name to benefit their desires and promote their self-rule. The country's president is a billionaire and is on the Forbes list, whereas his citizens are drinking the same water that they dispose of their wastes. May God help us.

Adorable Verses from
the Glorious Quran

T he following are a few verses from the Quran that I admire profoundly and would like to share with you. These jewels illuminate the divine guidance for humanity.

Success

Chapter 2, Verses 2-5

- This is the Book of Allah, and there is no doubt that it is a guidance for the pious;

- For those who believe in the existence of that which is beyond the reach of perception (unseen), who establish Prayer and spend out of what We have provided for them;

- Who believe in what has been revealed to you and what was revealed before you, and have firm faith in the Hereafter;

- These are on the true guidance from their Lord; these are truly successful.

Piety And Righteousness

Chapter 2, Verse 177

Righteousness is not only that you turn your faces towards the East or the West (in prayers), but it is also righteousness to :

- Believe in God, the Last Day (of judgment), the Angels, the (divine) Book, and the Messengers (of God);

- Spend your wealth and resources that you like so much, out of love for God, for your relatives, for orphans, for the (helpless and) needy, for travelers, for those who ask, and for the redemption of the captives (of debt);

- Be punctual with your prayers (Salats) and practice regular charity (Zakat);

- Fulfill the contracts and promises that you have made;

- Be firm and patient in pain, suffering, and adversity during times of struggle.

These are the people who are sincere, the people of truth, and the God-fearing.

The Commandments

Chapter 17, Verses 22-37

Your Lord has ordained that you shall obey none but Him.

- Be good to your parents. Should one or both of them reach old age in your lifetime, do not say to them any word of contempt, nor repel them. Talk to them courteously and respectfully, and take care of them with humility and kindness. Be very humble to them and pray to God: My Lord, have mercy on them just as they raised me with their love and affection when I was a child.

- Your Lord knows best as to what is in your hearts. If you are righteous, He will be forgiving to those who turn to Him again and again, seeking His mercy.

- Share your wealth and give their dues to relatives, the needy, and travelers. Do not overspend your wealth and resources senselessly, as this will be associated with the devil. The devil is ungrateful to his Lord. If you cannot assist them as your own resources are limited, and you are seeking the Lord's mercy with hope, then talk to them very gently and politely.

  Do not be stingy and a miser, but do not be extravagant either, as it may result in your own poverty and helplessness. Your Lord grants abundantly to whom He pleases and measures it in a just manner. He is aware of the conditions of His servants and observes them closely.

- Do not kill your children out of fear of poverty. We shall provide sustenance for them and for you. Of course, killing them is a great blunder.

- Do not get even close to a situation that would tempt you to commit adultery. It is a shameful act and an immoral way that opens the door to other evils.

- Do not kill anyone whom God has forbidden, except for just cause under the law. If anyone is killed unjustly, We have granted the right of retribution to his heir. But let him not carry his vengeance too far in killing the culprit by taking the law into his own hands. The rights of the victim are supported and protected by the law.

- Do not approach any orphan's property until he attains maturity, except with the good intention of improving it.

- Fulfill your pledges as you shall be accountable for your promises.

- Give full (total) measures when you measure out anything and weigh with an accurate and reliable scale. This is fair and will be the best in the end.

- Do not pursue or get involved in something nor follow anyone blindly in matters you do not know. The use of your ears, eyes, and heart will be accountable on the Day of Judgment.

- Do not walk arrogantly on this earth, for you can neither slash the ground nor attain the highest of the mountains.

All these and their evil aspects are hateful in the sight of your Lord.

Rewards According To Deeds

Chapter 2, Verse 62

- Surely those who believe, and those who are Jews, and the Christians, and the Sabians, whoever believes in Allah and the Last day and does good, shall have their reward from their Lord, and there is no fear for them, nor shall they grieve.

Chapter 5, Verse 69

- Indeed those who believe and those who are Jews and the Sabians and the Christians who believe in Allah and the last day and do good shall have no fear nor grieve.

Social Justice

Chapter 4, Verse 75

- And what is (the matter) with you that you fight not in the cause of Allah and (for) the oppressed among men, women, and children who say, "Our Lord, take us out of this city of oppressive people and appoint for us from Yourself a protector and appoint for us from Yourself a helper."

Chapter 4, Verse 135

- Stand up firmly for justice, as a witness to Allah, even as against yourselves or your parents or your kin, whether it be against rich or poor.

Chapter 90, Verses 13-17

- The Quran urges us to follow a higher ethical plane that "Is to free the slave, to feed at a time of hunger an orphaned relative or a poor person in distress, and to be one of those who believe and urge one another to steadfastness (in doing good) and compassion."

Social Behavior

Chapter 4, Verses 36 & 86

- Worship Allah, and do not associate with Him anything, and be good to parents and to kinsmen and orphans and the needy and the close neighbor and the distant neighbor and the companion at your side and the wayfarer and those who work under your command. Surely, Allah does not like those who are arrogant, or proud.

- When you meet each other, offer good wishes and blessings for safety. One who conveys to you a message of safety and security and also offers a courteous greeting, meet it with a greeting that is more courteous or (at least) of equal courtesy.

Chapter 31, Verses 18 & 19

- Do not turn your face away from people, and do not walk on this earth haughtily. Allah does not like anyone who is arrogant, or proud. Be moderate in your walk, and lower your voice. Surely, the ugliest of voices is the braying of the donkeys.

Chapter 49, Verses 9, 11 & 12

- And if two factions among the believers should fight, then make a settlement between the two. But if one of them oppresses the other, then fight against the one that oppresses until it returns to the ordinance of Allah. And if it returns, then make a settlement between them in justice and act justly. Indeed, Allah loves those who act justly.

- O you who have believed, let not a people ridicule (another) people; perhaps they may be better than them, nor let women ridicule (other) women; perhaps they may be better than them. And do not insult one another and do not call each other by [offensive] nicknames. Wretched is the name of disobedience after [one's] faith. And whoever does not repent - then it is those who are the wrongdoers.

- O you who have believed, avoid much (negative) assumption. Indeed, some assumption is sin. And do not spy or backbite each other. Would one of you like to eat the flesh of his brother when dead? You would detest it. And fear Allah; indeed, Allah is Accepting of repentance and Merciful.

News And Information

Chapter 17, Verse 36

- Do not blindly follow any information you have no direct knowledge of. (Using your faculties of perception and conception) you must verify it for yourself.

In the Court of your Lord, you will be held accountable for your hearing, sight, and faculty of reasoning.

Chapter 24, Verses 15 & 16

- If you do not have complete knowledge about anything, keep your mouth shut. You might think that speaking about something without full knowledge is trivial. But it might have grave consequences.

Chapter 49, Verse 6

- O you who have believed, if there comes to you a disobedient one with information, investigate, lest you harm people out of ignorance and become regretful over what you have done.

Sustenance

Chapter 2, Verse 164

- Indeed, in the creation of the heavens and earth, and the alternation of night and day, and the (great) ships which sail through the sea with that which benefits people, and what Allah has sent down from the heavens of rain, giving life thereby to the earth after its lifelessness and dispersing therein every (kind of) moving creature, and (His) directing of the winds and the clouds, that are controlled between the heaven and the earth, are signs for a people who use reason.

Chater6, Verse 99

- And it is He who sends down rain from the sky, and We produce thereby the growth of all things. From its greenery, we produce grains arranged in layers. And from the palm trees - of its emerging clusters of fruits hanging low. And (We produce) gardens of grape-vines and olives and pomegranates, similar yet varied. Look at (each of) its fruits when it yields and (at) it's ripening. Indeed that are signs for people who believe.

Chapter 14, Verse 32

- It is Allah Who created the heavens and the earth and sent down rain from the sky and produced thereby some fruits as provision for you and subjected for you the ships to sail through the sea by His command and subjected for you the rivers.

Chapter 15, Verses 20 & 22

- And We have made for you therein means of living and (for) those to whom you are not providers. And We have sent the fertilizing winds and sent down water from the sky and given you drink from it. And you are not its retainers.

Allah (Swt)

Chapter 24, Verse 35

- Allah is the Light of the heavens and the earth. The example of His light is like a niche within which is a lamp, the lamp is within the glass, the glass as if it were a pearly brilliant star lit from (the oil of) a blessed olive tree, neither of the East nor of the West, whose oil would almost glow even if untouched by fire. Light upon light. Allah guides His light to whom He wills. And Allah presents examples for the people, and Allah is Knowing of all things.

Chapter 59, Verses 22, 23 & 24

- He is Allah: there is no god but He; the Knower of the unseen and the manifest, He is the Most Merciful, the Most Compassionate.

- He is Allah: there is no god but He; the Sovereign, the Holy One, the Source of Peace (and Perfection), the Guardian of Faith, the Preserver of Safety, the Exalted in Might, the Irresistible, the Supreme: Glory to Allah! (High is He) above the partners, they attribute to Him.

- He is Allah, the Planner, Executer, and Fashioner of creation. His are the names most beautiful. Whatever is in the heavens and the earth extols His Glory. He is the Most Mighty, the Most Wise

Chapter 112, Verses 1-4

- Say: He is Allah, the One and Only. Allah is Independent of all and all are dependent on Him. Neither has He an offspring nor is He the offspring of anyone. And none is equal with Him in rank.

Dude, Where is my Religion?

During a past *Ramadan* in California, a Japanese lady asked her co-worker, a young Muslim man from India, "what did you guys achieve by staying all day without food and water?" The Muslim man explained to her that we not only stay away from food and drinks, but we also stay away from lying, cheating, hurting others, vulgarity, and other foul deeds. The Japanese lady replied in shock, "Oh my God, you guys are very fortunate. We have to stay away from these bad virtues for twelve months." Dude, where is my religion?

A Muslim went into the bathroom. Before entering, he recited the *Duaa* (supplication) for entering the bathroom. When he exited, he recited the *Duaa* for exiting the bathroom. After utilizing it, he left the bathroom in a total mess, dirty, filthy, and unusable for the next person: water on the floor, on the toilet seat, toilet tissues everywhere, and paper towels in the toilet. Dude, where is my religion?

On the 27th night of *Ramadan*, I stood up all night praying *Nafil Salats* (non-obligatory prayers)and reciting the *Quran*. After *Sahri* (breakfast before dawn), I offered *Fajar* (morning prayer)and realized that I was too sleepy and tired to go to work. I called my friend and asked him to forge my presence at the office. I knew that during *Ramadan*, they won't care for this lie, as we all do it. Dude, where is my religion?

During a recent Friday *Khutba (sermon)*, our Imam was preaching that we should never give up on Allah's mercy. He gave the example of a sinner who had committed 99 murders and then approached his Imam to pray for Allah's forgiveness. The Imam refused, and the guy killed him, thus making it 100. After this, the killer prayed directly to Allah to forgive all his sins, including 100 murders, and Allah accepted his *Duaa*. Following the *Salat* (prayer), I asked our Imam who this man was, during what period of history, and in what city he lived. He committed 100 murders and was never prosecuted and never paid for his heinous crimes. The Imam looked at me as I questioned his knowledge and wisdom and just walked away from me without answering. Dude, where is my religion?

My fellow worshiper at the Masjid looked at the vast number of men and women for Friday *Salat* and said, "*Insha Allah* (God willing), Islam will flourish again when we have this level of attendance for the *Fajar Salat* at dawn." I looked at the littered shoes at the Masjid entrance, the cars parked everywhere blocking others, and the dirty bathrooms with water on the floor, and I thought. Islam will flourish when we learn how to properly use the toilets, how to park the cars without blocking others, and when we place our shoes in the empty shoe racks. Dude, where is my religion?

We went to *Umrah (pilgrimage to Mecca)*. We lied about the age of our toddler to save on the airline ticket. I bribed the religious police inside *Masjid-e-Nabwi* (holy mosque in Medina) to hold a place for me in the first row. A friend told us that he reported a piece of missing luggage at Jeddah Airport and that lie paid for one family member's ticket. Muslims were crushing each other to reach the sacred Black Stone in the *Kaaba* (Mecca). My uncle performs Umrah in *Ramadan* each year to take care of his deeds for the remaining eleven months. My childhood friend has a written *Fatwa* (declaration) that states interest dealings permissible in business loans and home mortgages. He is a big donor and is on the Board of the local mosque. People are rushing not to be late for the non-obligatory *Taraweeh Salats*. After *Ramadan*, they don't even offer the mandatory *Isha Salat*. Dude, where is my religion?

The airport security searched a Muslim arrival and found a hand-made necklace hanging on his neck. He told the Immigration Officer that this was a "*Taweez*" from his mother to safeguard him during travel to the USA. The officer ripped it open and found some writings inside. He asked the man to explain the script. The Muslim man told the security officer that he could read it, but he did not know its translation. In response to the officer's disbelief, he further explained that, in his country, many people memorize the entire holy book *(Quran)* without knowing its meaning. Dude, where is my religion.

The Leader told me that the *Jamaat* (team) was heading to the *Masjid* (mosque) in the next city the next day, where they intended to continue *Dawah (preaching)*. The pathway between the two Masjids was filled with girls in skimpy clothes, bars selling alcohol, stores with pork on sale, and banks advertising high-interest rates. I saw the devil *(Shaytan)* looking happy and victorious. Man, I worked very hard for centuries to achieve this. Now the *Mullas* (clerics)are confined inside the Masjids, and I control the rest of the world. I allow gay marriages, adultery, alcohol, pork, *riba* (interest), nudity, abortion, you name it. They can not even call the *Azan* (call to pray) outside the walls of the Masjid. Dude, where is my religion?

The Imam has arrived just in time to deliver the Friday sermon. He is dressed in a spotless long white robe, well-groomed, wearing perfume, walking gracefully, smiling, and waving. He draws a salary of over $ 80,000 and performs only specific religious duties within limited hours. He delivers Khutbah (sermon) that Muslims should not celebrate Valentine's, Halloween, or birthdays. I never saw him assisting in managing parking, cleaning, food, or other matters in the Masjid. Maybe these tasks are not suitable for his dignified personality. However, he frequently gives examples of *Rashidun* Caliphs (seventh-century Muslim leaders). Dude, where is my religion?

Do you want to know the answer? It is very distinctly specified on the very first page of the Quran. Just read Verses 1 through 5 of the *Surat Buqra* (the second chapter of the

Quran). Read its meaning, read its *Tafseer* (explanation). Follow this single page of the Quran in your daily life, and you are guaranteed success in both worlds; this life, and the life after death.

HAJJ:
The Global Annual
Congregation of Muslims

Hajj is the pilgrimage to Mecca, and Muslims are obligated to make it at least once in their lifetime if they are healthy and can afford to do so. It represents a very high religious attainment and the spiritual apex of a Muslim's life, and to be the pilgrim of God is the dream of every Muslim. Over three million Muslim men and women, old and young, rich and poor, travel to Saudi Arabia each year to attend this annual congregation. This year, 2022, the 5-day global assembly of Muslims will take place in July.

Diversity, Equality, And Unity

The most magnificent characteristics of Hajj are the diversity, equality, and uniformity in Islam. All races and nationalities come together with tolerance and respect to demonstrate fairness and harmony. Islam has no place for discrimination, and Hajj provides a vivid display of this essential code.

Malcolm X, an American human rights activist, describes his experience at Hajj as follows: "There were tens of thousands of pilgrims from all over the world. They were of all colors, from blue-eyed blondes to black-skinned Africans. But we were all participating in the same ritual, displaying a spirit of unity and brotherhood. On this pilgrimage, what I have seen and experienced has forced me to re-arrange much of my thought patterns previously held."

Unity and oneness are the fundamental principles of Islam. Once a year, millions of Muslims elevate themselves from the differences in financial status, skin color, ethnicity, country of origin, social rank, and cultural pride. To show that all men are created equal, they stand together praising God, wearing only two pieces of unstitched white cloth, eliminating any obvious distinction. Their goal is to set aside their political, social, and other disagreements and endeavor for the spiritual unity of Islam.

In addition, Hajj is a great opportunity to mingle with other Muslims from various parts of the world. You can experience their traditions, admire their clothing, and enjoy their food. The tent next to yours may occupy Muslims from a small village in Turkey, from a remote town in Sudan, or from a big city in Australia.

The Impact Of Hajj

Hajj is a spiritual journey in which the human being tries to make a passionate and humble connection with the Creator. From the moment you make the intention to go to Hajj, an unseen bond is established between yourself and God. This bond reaches its peak in the enormous valley of Arafat on the second day of the 5-day event. The love for God inside you has become dormant over a lifetime of worldly trappings.

When you start preparing for your journey, this love takes over your heart, your eyes sparkle, and your face glows with intensity. Your thoughts and actions are changing. You seek forgiveness for your past mistakes and ask for God's refuge. You contact your family members, friends, and loved ones and ask for their forgiveness if you have offended anyone.

Leaving behind your assets, your family, your business, your job, and the comfort of your home, you are now on your way to walk on the grounds where prophets have walked before, and you are going to be face to face with and literally touching the Kaaba, the House of God. On this journey, you do not want to abuse anyone and will stay away from back-biting, rage, indecency, and arguments. You have been invited to the House of God, and only the chosen ones receive this honor. You are becoming a different person, peaceful, calm, and nice, who wants to do good to others and stay away from bad deeds. You are a pilgrim to God.

On the second day of Hajj, when you stand together with three million other Muslims in the valley of Arafat, by yourself, without any worldly attachment, with your hands spread above your head, asking for the forgiveness of God, the Creator connects with His creation and shower you with His blessings. You do not care about how big your house is or how much your bank account is. You are only crying for His mercy.

At the end of Hajj, you become a different person, with a new set of values, goals, and morals. You have just experienced a once-in-a-lifetime transformation, mentally, emotionally, and spiritually. You are proud to be a human being, and a devoted Muslim, who has just been in the attendance of God. Your view of worldly assets and pleasures has changed.

"Estimating the Impact of the Hajj: Religion and Tolerance in Islam's Global Gathering," a 2008 study conducted in conjunction with Harvard University's John F. Kennedy School of Government, found that the Hajj experience promotes peaceful coexistence, equality, and harmony among ethnic groups and the Islamic community.

Prophet's (pbuh) Last Sermon

Prophet Muhammad, peace be upon him, delivered his farewell sermon on the second day of Hajj in the valley of Mount Arafat on Friday, 6th March 632. It is a very renowned address to humanity and highlights the fundamental guidelines of Islam. Following is the English translation of a portion of this sermon.

"O People, just as you regard this month, this day, this city as Sacred, so regard the life and property of every Muslim as a sacred trust. Return the goods entrusted to you to their rightful owners. Hurt no one so that no one may hurt you. Remember that you will indeed meet your Lord and that He will indeed reckon your deeds.

Allah has forbidden you to take usury (interest). Therefore all interest obligations shall henceforth be waived. Your capital, however, is yours to keep. You will neither inflict nor suffer any inequity. Allah has judged that there shall be no interest and that all the interest due shall henceforth be waived.

O People, it is true that you have certain rights with regard to your women, but they also have rights over you. Remember that you have taken them as your wives only under Allah's trust and with His permission. If they abide by your right, then to them belongs the right to be fed and clothed in kindness. Do treat your women well and be kind to them, for they are your partners and committed helpers.

O People, listen to me in earnest, worship Allah, say your five daily prayers, fast during the month of Ramadan, and give your wealth in Zakat. Perform Hajj if you can afford to.

All mankind is from Adam and Eve, an Arab has no superiority over a non-Arab, nor a non-Arab has any superiority over an Arab; also, a white has no superiority over a black, nor does a black have any superiority over a white except by piety and good action.

Learn that every Muslim is a brother to every Muslim and that the Muslims constitute one brotherhood. Nothing should be legitimate to a Muslim which belongs to a fellow

Muslim unless it was given freely and willingly. Do not, therefore, do injustice to yourselves.

Remember, one day, you will appear before Allah and answer your deeds. So beware, do not stray from the path of righteousness after I am gone."

The Hypocrisy of Muslims

"Righteousness is not that you turn your faces toward the east or the west, but true righteousness is in one who believes in Allah, the Day of Judgment, the Angels, the Book, and the Prophets and gives his wealth, in spite of the love for it, to relatives, orphans, the needy, the traveler, those who ask for help, and for freeing enslaved people; and who establishes Prayer and gives Zakat; those who fulfill their promise and contracts when they are made; and those who are patient in tribulation and adversity and time of stress. Such are they who are sincere. Those are the ones who have been true, and it is those who are righteous." Quran (2-177).

This Verse of the Holy Quran mentions two kinds of holiness and righteousness, one that benefits only you and the other that helps the people all around you. The tragedy of Islam today is that most Muslims emphasize the first kind and do not place much importance on the second kind. This is the difference between Muslims suffering everywhere and non-believers who are on top of the world. And even the first kind of good deeds are performed as rituals and not ibadah.

Every year over three million Muslims from all over the world perform Hajj. They exhaust their life savings for this once-in-a-lifetime experience. Many of them face hardships of travel, and others spend their life savings. They go back to their homes carrying Zum-Zum (sacred water), dates, beads, and Itar (perfume). Men will grow beards, and women will start wearing hijab. After a few months, they will find themselves busy in the same life-routine full of worldly deceptions.

My question to you is, what have these people accomplished? **Is there an impact of this colossal global gathering of Muslims at one specified place and time? Has the Muslim world changed for the better after the Hajj?** What is the significance of Hajj? Circling Kaaba and stoning the devil? My dear friend, a renowned physician at Memorial Hospital, went on a pilgrimage a few years ago. I congratulated him for performing Hajj. He said, "Taj Bhai, what I just performed were a few rituals. My real Hajj will begin now. How much can I improve my life and the lives of others around me? Insha Allah."

Every week, at the end of the Friday Sermon, we hear the following: "Recite what has been revealed to you of the book and establish Salah. **Indeed, Salah prevents you from immoral sins and evil deeds.** It is the greatest act of praising Allah. Allah knows what you do." (Quran 29-45). Of course, the way we offer Salah will not prevent us from immoral sins and evil doings. Even our religious leaders and teachers are involved in such acts. I have just read a report about sexual harassment of Muslim women in the Kaaba during the Tawaf. The predators are Muslim men who are there performing Hajj. One of the largest brothels in the world is located in a Muslim country, where sewers are routinely clogged due to the overwhelming number of condoms flushed down the toilets.

Salah is our direct contact with Allah. We do stand in His audience, thanking and praising Him. We focus our minds on this audience and avoid thinking about earthly items. "Indeed, Salah is an obligatory duty that should be performed at prescribed times by the believers." (Quran 4-19). Salah teaches us punctuality. Salah creates a well-defined structure of a Muslim's daily activities. A typical day is divided into four segments, morning, afternoon, evening, and night. Each part starts with performing a Salah. For each component of the day, we present ourselves in front of our Creator. We obey, praise, and be grateful to the Almighty. After this obligation, we get busy with the scheduled worldly activities for this part of the day. Our activities for the entire day (and night) should be scheduled around the prescribed times for the five Salah.

What I described above is the significance of Salah. Now let me tell you how I execute this extremely important duty of my religion. I am happy and satisfied with my Fajar Salah. However, the other four Salah are accomplished without any magnitude. To begin with, I do not understand what I am reading in my Namaz, as I don't know the Arabic Language. I enact the prescribed physical movements and recite memorized verses from the Quran. My brain cannot focus as it is wandering all over the place. I fail to understand that I am standing in front of my Lord, my Creator. I do forget whether it is the third Rakat or the fourth. I treat my Salah as a part of my daily tasks without any importance. It just becomes a routine as I must do it five times a day, every day of my adult life. As soon as I finish the Salah, I am back into all ill-doings.

The Friday Prayer has become a formality. Over 50% will miss the obligatory Khutbah and arrive just before the Faraz Namaz. The Imam mentions events that happened centuries ago. He does not give any example of a living person. Today Muslims do not have a role model living among us. Not a single example. We have to travel back for centuries to look for one. The Imam does not mention the conditions of Muslims around the world. During the past Hajj, the Saudi Imam refused to make Duaa for Muslims in the Indian Occupied Kashmir.

The sermon never talks about the future. The audience is not paying any attention. They want to fulfill this formality and depart immediately. I genuinely believe that if we were allowed to pray Jumma at home, then the attendance would be less than half. Is this the weekly assembly prescribed by our religion? Is this the obligation that is mentioned in the Quran? Whom are we kidding? Ourselves or our Lord? Shame on us.

Salah teaches us discipline and organization. To offer Salah in the congregation, we form straight lines and follow Imam. However, this discipline is observed only during Faraz Salah. An ex-defense minister of Israel once said that he is afraid of the day when Arabs will learn how to form and stand in lines. Time magazine once wrote about Muslims: no discipline and no organization; and no leadership and no unity. The chaotic scene at the Black Stone at Kaaba is the worst display of discipline in Muslims.

The congregation provides us the means to get together five times a day and bond with other Muslims. The goal is to develop a Muslim community that can provide guidance and assistance and address issues facing our families. We go to Masjid to offer our prayers in the congregation only because the reward is 27 times more than if we pray Salah at home. We care about our rewards, and we do not care about the community.

In 2010, the Global Economy Journal published a comprehensive study, "How Islamic are the Islamic Countries?" It was co-authored by Professors Scheherazade Rehman and Hossein Askari, both from George Washington University, Washington, DC. Out of 208 rankings, New Zealand is on top of the list, Canada 7, the UK 8, Australia 9, Germany 17, France 18, and the USA 25.

Not a single Muslim country is in the top 37 places. The rankings of major Muslim countries are Malaysia 38, Turkey 103, Saudi Arabia 131, Indonesia 140, Pakistan 147, Bangla Desh 152, Egypt 153, Iran 163, Afghanistan 169, Syria 186, Libya 196, and Somalia 206.

In 2021 The World Justice Project released the rankings of 139 Judicial Systems in the world. Not a single Muslim country was listed among the top 30 places.

I am showing you a mirror. Please face yourself and try to improve. Try to attain the fundamental goals and true purpose of the foundation and the five pillars of Islam. May Allah help us and guide us. Aameen. I will leave you with the following message about the Holy Quran. It was written some 35 years ago by the ninth President of India, Dr. Pandit Shanker Dayal Sharma.

It was a command for action. You turned it into a book of prayer.

It was a book to understand. You read it without understanding.

It was a code for the living. You turned it into a manifesto of the dead.

That which was a book of knowledge; You abdicated to the ignoramus.

It came to give knowledge of Creation. You abandoned it to the madrassah.

It came to give life to dead nations. You used it for seeking mercy for the dead.

O' Muslims! What have you done?

The Foundation of Islam

An abundance of books and volumes of literature have been written and spoken about the five pillars of Islam, Tauheed, Salat, Roza, Zakat, and Hajj. However, I have seldom seen valuable discussions about the foundation of Islam, the basic foundation on which the entire structure of our Deen is built. The system instituted upon it may not be strong and stable if the foundation is not sturdy and durable. The first five Ayats of Surat Baqarah define Succuss and who are the Successful. It describes the Foundation of Islam on the first page as a pre-qualification to read the Quran.

Islam is founded on two major components :

- Faith and Belief in the Unseen

- Utmost, and absolute certainty in the Hereafter.

Verses 2 to 5 of Chapter 2 of the Quran

- This is the Book of Allah, and there is no doubt that it is a guidance for the pious;

- For those who believe in the existence of that which is beyond the reach of perception (unseen), who establish Prayer and spend out of what We have provided for them;

- Who believe in what has been revealed to you and what was revealed before you, and have firm faith in the Hereafter;

- These are on the true guidance from their Lord; these are truly successful.

Faith and Belief in the Unseen

Our Deen requires that we MUST have total and complete faith and belief in the unseen. The unseen implies those realities which are hidden, concealed, invisible, or unknown, and cannot be perceived by our senses and cannot be experienced directly through human experience and observation. Having faith in a vast, unseen world that our sense of perception cannot comprehend is a requirement for having faith in Allah, such as the Being and Attributes of Allah, Angels, Revelation, Heaven, Hell, etc. It also includes future events that only Allah knows. To obtain guidance from the Quran, one must believe in the unseen.

We must place our total faith and complete trust in the messages from our Prophets as we follow the instructions from the experts in various fields in this physical world. Only such a person who believes in the "unseen" can attain the utmost, precious, and maximum benefits from the Guidance of the Quran. The one who believes only in those entities that can be seen, tasted and smelt, or measured and weighed may not be able to achieve valuable and proper guidance from this Book.

Belief in the unseen is the first essential quality of a believer. It is the foundation of our Deen and is the basis of all the roots and branches of religion. Although intellect and understanding are essential in Islam, without belief in the unseen, there can be no faith. To reject all that is unseen is to deny our belief.

Hereafter: Judgement and Accountability

Islam requires that we MUST have the utmost and absolute certainty, and without a shred of doubt in the Hereafter, in the Akhirah, and our life after death. Akhirah is the term used in Islam to describe the belief in everlasting life after death. According to Islam, death is not the end of life but a transfer from this world to the immortal world. Life on Earth is a test from Allah to prepare us for eternal life. More importantly, the Quran tells us that Allah will not test us beyond our limits. This Statement encourages Muslims to take responsibility for their actions. Akhirah is necessary so that true justice can be administered. In this world, pious persons suffer and do not reap a full reward for their efforts. Similarly, evil people triumph and often do not receive full punishment for their deeds. Allah, who is Just, wants full justice to be done and everyone to be fully indemnified.

The Quran shows us that there will come a day when the entire universe will be shattered. On this day, called the Day of Judgement, the dead will be resurrected for judgment by Allah. All humans will receive Allah's reward or punishment according to their beliefs and actions. We may enter Paradise by living according to the teachings of the Quran. Therefore, obeying the rules set by Allah is of the utmost importance to us. If there is no Judgment Day, we can do as we please with no consequence for our actions. According to the Quran, the present world is not an eternal abode. It tells us that man is placed here only temporarily so that Allah may test the moral fiber in terms of his obedience to Allah's will. He must never forget that there will be life hereafter or Akhirah. There is a time limit to his mortal existence. Death marks the end of the testing period for all human beings. But death only means a change of abode, for the soul never dies. The man returns to the realm from whence he came so that he may wait for Judgement Day. That realm, the life hereafter, is the eternal world. Thus, a human being's life is divided into two parts: a brief pre-death period of test and an eternal life in the post-death period of the world of the Hereafter.

It is very easy to lose sight of the Akhirah or fail to be fully conscious of this most important reality. It is easy to forget that we will harvest in the Akhirah what we sow in this world and that, for good or for bad, we are all engaged in planting each moment of our present life. There are several reasons for this loss of sight and forgetfulness. We do not see the Akhirah before our eyes as we do other things. We have no experience of it. And, of course, we have many distractions. The vivid and variety-filled world we see before our eyes attract and occupy our attention, time, and energy. This world seems solid and permanent, while death seems remote and the Akhirah merely an abstract proposition of no immediate relevance.

A Word of Caution

My dear brothers and sisters in Islam, please pay attention. If you do not have firm faith in the Unseen, or you do not have absolute certainty in the Hereafter, then your structure of Deen is built on a shaky foundation. A minor disturbance in the grounds of your life can easily damage this structure. The Deen becomes a collection of stories, historical events, and doubtful predictions. As soon as you exit the Masjid, you jump back into worldly distractions and illicit activities. This is the root cause of the downfall of Muslims worldwide, and it is happening today right here in front of our eyes.

Precious Words of
the Prophet Muhammad (pbuh)
Should be known to Muslims and Non-Muslims

Letter to the Greek Orthodox Monks

The Greek Orthodox monks living in the monastery at the foot of Mount Sinai have in their possession many precious documents going back many centuries. Their library is one of the finest in the world for ancient manuscripts. One of the most precious documents is the copy of a letter narrated by Prophet Muhammad (pbuh) to the monks in the year 628. Its contents might surprise many since in this precious manuscript Muslims are urged and encouraged to protect the Christians living within their midst. The words are so beautiful that we repeat them in full here.

In 628 C.E., Prophet Muhammad (pbuh) granted a Charter of Privileges to the monks of St. Catherine Monastery in

Mount Sinai. It consisted of several clauses covering all aspects of human rights, including the protection of Christians, freedom of worship and movement, freedom to appoint their choice of judges and to own and maintain their property, exemption from military service, and the right to protection in war. Following is the English translation.

" This is a message from Muhammad Ibn Abdullah, as a covenant to those who adopt Christianity, near and far, we are with them.

Verily I, the servants, the helpers, and my followers defend them because Christians are my citizens; and by Allah! I hold out against anything that displeases them. No compulsion is to be on them. Neither are their judges to be removed from their jobs nor their monks from their monasteries.

No one is to destroy a house of their religion, damage it, or carry anything from it to the Muslims' houses.

Should anyone take any of these, he would spoil God's covenant and disobey His Prophet. Verily, they are my allies and have my secure charter against all that they hate. No one is to force them to travel or oblige them to fight. The Muslims are to fight for them.

If a female Christian is married to a Muslim, it is not to occur without her approval. She is not to be prevented from visiting her church to pray.

Their churches are to be respected. They are neither to be prevented from repairing them nor the sacredness of their covenants.

No one of the nation (Muslims) is to disobey the covenant till the Last Day (end of the world)"

The Farewell Sermon

The Farewell Sermon, also known as Muhammad's Final Sermon or the Last Sermon, is a religious speech delivered by the Prophet Muhammad on Friday the 9th of Dhu al-Hijjah, 10 A.H. (6 March 632) in the Uranah valley of Mount Arafat, during the Islamic pilgrimage of Hajj. Following is the English translation.

"O People, lend me an attentive ear, for I know not whether, after this year, I shall ever be amongst you again. Therefore listen to what I am saying to you very carefully and take these words to those who could not be present here today.

O People, just as you regard this month, this day, this city as Sacred, so regard the life and property of every Muslim as a sacred trust. Return the goods entrusted to you to their rightful owners. Hurt no one so that no one may hurt you. Remember that you will indeed meet your Lord and that He will indeed reckon your deeds. Allah has forbidden you to take usury (interest); therefore, all interest obligations shall henceforth be waived. Your capital, however, is yours to keep. You will neither inflict nor suffer any inequity. Allah has judged that there shall be no interest and that all the interest due to Abbas ibn Abdul Muttalib (the Prophet's uncle) shall henceforth be waived.

Beware of Satan for the safety of your religion. He has lost all hope that he will ever be able to lead you astray in big things, so beware of following him in small things.

O People, it is true that you have certain rights concerning your women, but they also have rights over you. Remember that you have taken them as your wives only under Allah's trust and with His permission. If they abide by your right, then to them belongs the right to be fed and clothed in kindness. Treat your women well and be kind to them, for they are your partners and committed helpers. And it is your right that they do not make friends with anyone of whom you do not approve, as well as never to be unchaste.

"O People, listen to me in earnest, worship Allah, perform your five daily prayers (salah), fast during the month of Ramadan, and give your wealth in zakat. Perform Hajj if you can afford it.

All mankind is from Adam and Eve. An Arab has no superiority over a non-Arab, nor a non-Arab has any superiority over an Arab; also, a white has no superiority over a black, nor does a black have any superiority over a white, except by piety and good action.

Learn that every Muslim is a brother to every Muslim and that all Muslims constitute one brotherhood. Nothing shall be legitimate to a Muslim which belongs to a fellow Muslim unless it was given freely and willingly. Do not, therefore, do injustice to yourselves.

Remember, one day, you will appear before Allah and answer for your deeds. So beware, do not stray from the path of righteousness after I am gone.

O People, no prophet or apostle will come after me, and no new faith will be born. Reason well, therefore, O People, and understand words which I convey to you. I leave behind me two things, the Quran and my example, the Sunnah, and if you follow these, you will never go astray.

All those who listen to me shall pass on my words to others and those to others again, and may the last ones understand my words better than those who listen to me directly. Be my witness, O Allah, that I have conveyed your message to your people".

May Allah allow us to reflect and act upon the advice of the beloved Prophet (PBUH). May He enable our hearts to be nourished in His love and empower us to learn and follow the Sunnah as a means to fulfilling His command. Ameen. Peace be upon Prophet Muhammad. He is truly a mercy to humankind.

Can You Hear The Screams Of Your Sister? She Is Calling On You And Me. Where Are Her Spineless And Shameless Muslim Brothers?

Contributions by Brother Javed Qureshi and Imam Amo Jaffar who visited the refugee camps in Bangladesh and interviewed the victims. The material in this article is also adopted from a report by Shashank Bengali, Ukhia, Bangladesh, June 2018.

She relives the nightmare when she sees the boy lying in her arms. He is an innocent reminder of the day last year when soldiers burst into her village in western Myanmar's Rakhine state and chased her into a rice paddy. There, she said, two men in army uniforms raped her and left her bleeding in the dirt. Uma Suleiman said that soldiers, recognizable in their green uniforms with red patches, stormed the village one afternoon, scattering residents into the surrounding fields. When two soldiers caught up to her and drew a knife, no one was around to hear her cries. Villagers didn't find her until after nightfall.

Another victim Majida Begum, 23, said she was raped by soldiers in the woods outside her village in August. Fatima, 25, said she was gang-raped by half-a-dozen soldiers last June in the Maungdaw district. During a recent visit to the refugee camp, one woman told the Imam of Muttaqeen Masjid that her daughter was raped by 20 soldiers in front of her family.

Uma Suleiman is a widow and, at age 30, had already borne five children whom she was raising by herself in the sprawling Balukhali refugee camp. She is one of the thousands of Rohingya Muslims who were sexually assaulted during a systematic campaign of brutality by Myanmar security forces. International investigators and human rights groups have described these assaults as crimes against humanity. In the overcrowded refugee camps in Bangladesh, more than 900,000 Rohingya Muslims have sought shelter. Many have watched their homes burned, children mutilated, and family members shot. The mass rapes have produced untold numbers of unwanted pregnancies and confronted survivors with a terrible choice.

Tucked away in the shadows of her family's bamboo shelter, the girl hid from the world. She was 13, and she was petrified. Two months earlier, soldiers had broken into her home back in Myanmar and raped her, an attack that drove her and her terrified family over the border to Bangladesh. Ever since then she had waited for her period to arrive. Gradually, she came to realize that it would not. For the girl, a Rohingya Muslim who agreed to be identified by only her first initial, A, the pregnancy was a prison she was desperate to escape. The rape itself had destroyed her innocence. But carrying the baby of a Buddhist soldier could destroy her life.

According to Human Rights Watch, Myanmar forces also raided several Rohingya villages in June 2017, the month Uma Suleiman said she was raped. Sexual violence has been a devastating hallmark of Myanmar's long persecution of the Rohingya, forced by the Buddhist majority to live under apartheid in their native land. Authorities in Myanmar have denied the Rohingya fundamental rights, including regular access to medical care. Many rape survivors remain unaware of treatment options even when they reach the relative safety of the refugee camps.

The United Nations and humanitarian agencies recorded more than 6,000 incidents of gender-based violence against Rohingya Muslims in a seven-month period beginning in late August 2017. That was the month the Myanmar army, responding to Rohingya militant attacks against police posts, launched deadly "clearance operations" that drove nearly 700,000 people from their homes, one of the greatest exoduses in modern times.

"Rape with impunity has been the characteristic of the attacks on Rohingya women and girls for years," said Matthew Smith, co-founder of Fortify Rights, an advocacy group that extensively studied Myanmar. "Soldiers used rape as a tool in a larger attack to destroy at least part of the Rohingya population. In legal terms, we're in the landscape of genocide." From August 2017 through April 2018, Doctors Without Borders treated 377 survivors of sexual violence — including girls as young as 7 — at hospitals and health posts across the camps. The group believes this is a fraction of the total number of victims.

Can you hear these screams from Rohingya Muslim women? No, we don't. We don't want to hear their callings. These cries disrupt our comfortable living and become unbearable for our happy and easy-going routines. Muslim women have become the easiest and the softest targets worldwide. WHY??? Because no one is here to stand up for them. All we do is go to another banquet to hear the conditions of these victims. We don't care that we have to answer for our actions one day. Dear sisters, your Muslim brothers have become spineless and shameless. You can NOT count on your men anymore. They have lost their courage and their dignity. You have to stand up, face the violence and fight these attackers yourself. Let us see what Allah and His Prophet (pbuh) are saying:

Quran: Surah Al-Nisa, 4:75: "And what is (the matter) with you that you fight not in the cause of Allah and (for) the oppressed among men, women, and children who say, "Our Lord, take us out of this city of oppressive people and appoint for us from Yourself a protector and appoint for us from Yourself a helper?"

Hadeeth: the Prophet (pbuh) said: "The People will soon summon one another to attack you as people when eating invite others to share their food." Someone asked, "Will that be because of our small numbers at that time?" He replied, "No, you will be numerous at that time: but you will be froth and scum like that carried down by a torrent (of water), and Allah will take the fear of you from the breasts (hearts) of your enemy and cast al-Wahn into your hearts." Someone asked, "O Messenger of Allah, what is al-wahn?" He replied, "Love of the world and dislike of death." (An authentic hadith recorded by Abu Dawud and Ahmad)

Many NGOs are working in the refugee camps in Bangladesh. I am listing only three such organizations. Please support them.

- BASMAH 561-945-3313,
- Friends of Humanity 954-693-0620,
- Doctors Without Borders 212-679-6800.

Forgive Those
Who Have Hurt Us

One of the distinguishing features of Ramadan is Forgiveness. The Prophet (pbuh) explained in one Hadith that Ramadan is a month whose beginning is mercy, the middle is forgiveness, and the end is freedom from hellfire. This makes it a great time to ask Allah for His Forgiveness. It's also an excellent time to open our hearts and cleanse them of grudges and bitterness by forgiving others. What better way to seek this divine forgiveness than by forgiving those who have wronged and hurt us? Just as we seek forgiveness from Allah, we must learn to forgive ourselves. When the servant knowingly gives up things and acts that nullify the fast, despite his ability to reach them in secret, he gives indeed strong evidence of his confident belief that Allah, the Almighty, watches over him in both his manifest and secret deeds. There is no doubt that this kind of conduct is a significant training to strengthen faith in Allah.

The Prophet (pbuh) said: "It is not permissible for a Muslim to abandon his brother (or sister) for more than three days, each of them turning away when they meet. The better of them is the one who gives the greeting of Salaam first." When Nelson Mandela became President of the Rainbow Nation, he said to his white and black fellows: "Forgiveness liberates the soul, it removes fear. That's why it's such a powerful weapon".

Forgiveness requires an extraordinary struggle against the bruised ego. And the bigger the hurt, the more difficult it is to forgive. Forgiving is giving up your right to hate or hurt the person who hurts you. Hate hurts you physically, mentally, and emotionally. Forgiveness gives you peace, tranquility, and happiness. During Ramadan, the doors of Allah's Mercy and Forgiveness are open. Allah described the believers and said: "And those who avoid the major sins and immoralities, and when they are angry, they forgive." (Quran 42:37). How can we raise our hands and ask Allah for Forgiveness but not be willing to forgive another human being?

The Prophet Muhammad (pbuh) said that Musa (pbuh), the son of Imran, once asked, "Oh my Lord! Who is the most honorable of Your servants?" And He replied, "the person who forgives even when he is in a position of power." Peace and blessings are upon the Prophet. When he entered the city of Makkah after the victory, the Prophet (pbuh) had some of his staunchest enemies in front of him. Those who fought him for many years persecuted his followers and killed many of them. Now he had full power to do whatever he wanted to punish them for their crimes. It is reported that the Prophet (pbuh) asked them, "What do you think I shall do to you now?" They pleaded for mercy. "No blame on you today. Go, you are all free." Subhan Allah, soon thereafter, they all came and accepted Islam due to his colossal act of mercy.

Once when the Prophet Muhammad (pbuh) was sitting in the Mosque with a group of his companions, he caught everyone by surprise by stating that the next person to enter the sanctuary would be a person of paradise. The Prophet's companions waited eagerly to see who it would be. Finally, a relatively simple man by the name of Abu Dumdum appeared. The companions were puzzled because they didn't think this person was extraordinarily pious.

One of the companions asked Abu Dumdum if he could stay with him for a few nights, making an excuse of need. In reality, he just wanted to know what was so special about Abu Dumdum. In the night, the companion expected Abu Dumdum to pray all night, but no such thing happened. During the day, the companion expected Abu Dumdum to fast, but that didn't happen either. Finally, the companion told Abu Dumdum what the Prophet (pbuh) had said and why he was spending nights in his home. Abu Dumdum replied that the only thing he did that was different and unique was before going to bed every night; he would forgive anyone who had offended him knowingly or unknowingly and go to sleep with a clean heart toward others.

Forgiveness in the Arabic language is related to the word "covering." When Allah (Mighty and Sublime) forgives

His servants' sins, those sins are covered on their books of evil deeds as if they never took place. Hence when believers filled with compassion truly forgive those who have wronged them, they cover up in their hearts the wrong that was done to them, not bringing those wrongs up to brow-beat people with later or to use as leverage against them. Sincere forgiveness is not to harbor hatred against those who have done us wrong. Having mercy for others is not punishing them when provided with such an opportunity. Forgiving those who have wronged us benefits the merciful. There's a deep sense that the way we treat others is how God will treat us. In other words, if we wish for Allah's gentle treatment, we must be gentle toward others.

We are not physical beings exclusively. We are spiritual beings housed in a physical container. The physical body has its life, and we have obligations to it, but it will be left behind. We can't let this physical body dominate the narrative. Although we tend to think of the mind, body, and spirit as separate components, in reality, they are all connected and interrelated, and improvement in any one naturally affects improvement in the others. Forgiving in Ramadan purifies the mind, body, and spirit, leading to greater clarity, sensitivity, and health.

This Ramadan, let's try and forgive everyone who has hurt us. It shows strength, self-confidence, and a desire to be forgiven by Allah. Let us forgive our parents, spouses, siblings, relatives, friends, and co-workers. Forgiveness is not easy, but boy is it worth it! And this is a reflection of the Qur'anic advice: "...pardon and forgive. Do you not wish that Allah should forgive you?" (24:22).

Muslims Killing Muslims

I want to tell you about two brothers. One is filthy rich with ample resources, very powerful, an arrogant dictator, living in a huge palace. The other bother is very poor with some farmland to support his family, gracious and hardworking. For years they lived next to each other in harmony and peace. Now they are fighting, and the rich brother is killing the poor brother and destroying his livelihood. It is happening right now, in front of us, openly and without remorse. We are enjoying the show from the sidelines, and nobody wants to stop the rich brother from this destruction.

Since March 2015, the Saudi war on Yemen has cost the lives of more than 12,000 civilians, including over 2,500 children and close to 2,000 women. The bombings have also wounded over 20,000 Yemeni civilians, while more than four million others have been displaced. Saudi air strikes had razed 270 medical centers, 25 media institutes, more than

400,000 houses, and over 700 mosques. Armed with American and British ammunitions, European warplanes, and Western-supported military hardware, for the past two years, the Kingdom has launched a destruction campaign against the impoverished country. And we are enjoying the show from the sidelines.

The devastation of civilian infrastructure plus restrictions on food and fuel imports have also pushed Yemen to the brink of famine. Millions are severely food insecure. About 3.3 million children and pregnant or breastfeeding women, including 462,000 children under five are facing severe acute malnutrition. People have been forced to drink untreated water, resulting in an outbreak of cholera and acute watery diarrhea, with over 22,000 sick and over 100 deaths. Millions lack access to primary healthcare. A child under five dies in Yemen every 10 minutes from preventable diseases.

According to a U.N. report released in 2016, it is believed that the coalition led by Saudi Arabia could be deliberately targeting civilians. Planes have bombarded a camp for displaced people, a dairy factory, civilian gatherings and weddings, civilian vehicles and buses, civilian residential areas, medical facilities, schools, mosques, markets, factories, food storage warehouses, and other essential civilian infrastructure. "Doctors without Borders," reports that it was attacked four times in three months by coalition forces.

Saudi Arabia is the primary destination for U.S. arms sales, purchasing nearly 10 percent of U.S. exports from 2011 to 2015. In May 2017, the United States sealed a multibillion-dollar arms deal with Saudi Arabia, worth $350 billion over ten years and $110 billion that will take effect immediately. The Obama administration offered over $115 billion of weapons to Saudi Arabia. American leaders are far-sighted and take steps that are in the best interests of their country. It will have a positive impact on our economy and will create hundreds of jobs.

Following are a few more examples of our "accomplishments" in 2016 & 2017.

- On February 16, 2017, ISIS claimed responsibility for a car bomb in southwestern Baghdad that killed 51 people and wounded at least as many others.

- On February 4, 2017, two suicide car bombs killed 53 people in the Syrian village of Susiyan and another eight a few hours later.

- On December 31, 2016, at least 28 people were killed and 50 wounded in a double bombing in Baghdad.

- On November 24, 2016, at least 80 people, many of them Shiite pilgrims on their way home to Iran, were killed when an ISIS suicide bomber detonated a truck filled with explosives at a roadside service station in southern Iraq.

- On September 10, 2016, 12 people were killed and more than 40 wounded in two suicide bombings at a shopping mall in Baghdad.

- On August 22, 2016, more than 50 people were killed and scores more wounded in a suicide attack at a wedding ceremony in Turkey's southeastern province of Gaziantep, near the Syrian border.

- On July 14, 2016, a suicide truck bomb ripped through a busy shopping district in Baghdad, killing more than 200, including at least 25 children and 20 women

The above are just a few examples of Muslims killing and destroying their Muslim brothers. Millions of Muslims have been killed by other Muslims in Iraq, Syria, Iran, Pakistan, and many other Muslim countries. What is our obligation? The Quran clearly tells us: "If two parties of believers quarrel, make peace between them" (49:7). However, have you seen any of our political or religious leaders getting involved and trying to mediate peace?

Have you ever heard our Imams mention this in our Juma Khutba? Our solution is to perform another pilgrimage, memorize the holy book (without understanding it), attend elaborate iftar parties, organize conferences in air-conditioned halls, deliver impact-less speeches, and follow symbolic acts, traditions, and rituals. Islam in the USA has become an academic religion with no unity and no national leadership.

The Muslim Character

On today's global horizon, every nation and religion has an image based on how others see them. Marketing has become as important as the substance itself. The Muslims may have good individual qualities, but collectively, we have developed an unpleasant character as a Jamat of 1.5 billion people. We are portrayed as being terrorists, honor-killers, unjust to our women, led by dictators and religious hardliners, poor, uncivilized, and on and on. The main reason is that we are developing a Muslim character that is dominated by symbolic and superficial elements instead of the core substance that is termed by our holy book as Eeman (faith). This character should be based on our Niyats (intentions) and our actions, instead of our appearance and our talks. Let me share with you some of my personal experiences.

Although this happened over two decades ago, it is still fresh in my mind. It was a late summer night, and I was returning from a family get-together. Coming down from Sunrise to Pembroke Pines, I was stopped by the Police at a checkpoint for DUI. The street was lighted with blue flashing lights on top of police cars, and we were directed to pull over and park behind a long line of cars. The cops were checking each car and each driver to see who had been drinking alcohol or maybe enjoying drugs. My wife was with me in the front seat, and my three children, 3, 7 & 8, were half-sleep in the back seat. I turned off the car engine and sat in my car, at 2 AM, knowing that it was going to be a long night. Very soon, a police officer came to our car and started asking questions as to where we were coming from and if we had been drinking. Suddenly the supervisor interrupted him, leaned into the car, looked at my family, and asked me, "Sir, are you a Muslim?" I said yes. He then turned to the first officer and told him to, "let them go. They are Muslims, and they don't drink." I was pulled out of the line and was allowed to leave. This is what I call a Muslim character. Once a non-Muslim knows that you are a Muslim, that should satisfy that person or that group, and they don't need to ask any further questions.

About ten years ago, I was visiting Chicago to attend a wedding ceremony. The next day I went to Dewan Avenue to do some shopping for my wife and children, who were in Florida. I was looking for a good sari for my wife when something in the store caught my eyes. A fine-looking life-size mannequin was dressed in a superb two-tone silk sari with vivid colors and dazzling embroidery work. I fell in love with that sari and decided to buy it for my beautiful wife. I expressed my desire to the shop owner, a sophisticated Muslim lady of Pakistani origin. She looked for that specific sari in a new and sealed package but was unable to find it. However, the same sari was available in other color combinations. Nothing else appealed to me, and I requested her to sell me the sari on the mannequin. What happened next was the true definition of the Hijab. Before removing the sari from the mannequin, the lady asked her two young assistants to bring a large plain sheet of cloth and create a screen between myself and the mannequin. After removing the sari behind the screen, they properly covered the mannequin with that large sheet of cloth. She did not want to undress the female figure of the mannequin in the presence of a strange male. She dignified that lifeless non-human female statue with a Hijab and refused to expose it to a stranger. At that moment, I discovered the true meaning of the Hijab and how this is the top-most characteristic of Muslim women. May Allah bless that honorable Muslim woman.

My children are now grown, married, and well settled with their families in their own homes. However, when they were young and still living at home with us, they experienced several Ramadans with their parents, and Sahur (breakfast before dawn) and Iftar (dinner after sunset) times were really busy. I used to get up early and wake up my wife to allow us a couple of hours to prepare and eat Sahur. My routine was to perform wudu and start the Tahajud Salats (non-obligatory night prayers). On the other hand, my wife would go to the kitchen and start cooking the food. During cooking, she would run between the kitchen and the bedrooms to try to wake up our three teenage children. She would push them into the bathroom to make themselves ready for the Sahur. By the time I was done with my Tahajjud Salaat, the food was prepared, and the children were ready to start the Sahur. We all ate together and then prepared for Fajar (morning) Salat. One day, after the Fajar Salat, I invited my children to sit down with me for a few minutes. I told them about my Tahajjud Salats and their mother's running around during Suhur. And then I asked them who was more righteous, who was more religious, and who was earning the better reward. Then I told them very clearly, that their mother's deeds were far, far better than my Nafil (non-obligatory) Salats. She was devoting her time to helping others, helping her family, and helping her children. Whereas my actions only benefitted me. I decided my Nafils to be more important than helping others. This is not the teaching of our religion. I explained Verse 177 of Chapter Two Al-Baqra of our holy book. A true Muslim will always prefer to help others and give it more importance than his own benefits, even his own Nafil Salats. This is the Muslim character.

I have shared three of my very personal experiences and will be glad to share more. May Allah bless all of us with a good and solid Muslim Character. Insha Allah (God willing), we will again see the day when non-Muslims will bring their disputes and concerns to us for our just advice and fair judgment. Ameen.

Chapter 2, Verse 177 of the Holy Quran

Righteousness is not only that you turn your faces towards east or west (in prayers), but it is also righteousness to :

- Believe in God, the Last Day (of judgment), the Angels, the (divine) Book, and the Messengers (of God);

- Spend your wealth and resources that you like so much, out of love for God, for your relatives, for orphans, for the (helpless and) needy, for the travelers, for those who ask, and for the redemption of the captives (of debt);

- Be punctual with your prayers (Salats) and practice regular charity (Zakat);

- Fulfill the contracts and promises that you have made;

- Be firm and patient in pain, suffering, and adversity during times of struggle.

These are the people who are sincere, the people of truth, and the God-fearing.

A Tale of Two Women

Note: The following article is not my original writing. I adopted most of it from various sources on the internet. Some names are changed to preserve discretion. This is the story of two women who are thousands of miles apart from each other, in different countries. They are from different cultures, and they follow different religions. However, they both are the victims of their orthodox cultural faith, and perhaps their gender also plays a role.

Letter from Israel

My name is Raia Tessler, and I live in Tel Aviv. I am now 64. For the past 28 years, I have been pleading with justice to get a divorce from my husband, but he will not give his permission. Under the court's interpretation of Jewish religious law, a husband's consent is necessary to end a marriage. As has been the case for centuries, a Jewish divorce is not final in

Israel until the men deliver handwritten divorce decrees into the cupped hands of the women. Even if you're not religious, you have to be divorced by Jewish religious law that governs family matters.

An Israeli woman can't split from her spouse without proving extraordinary abuse or neglect. A simple assertion of "We don't get along" or "This marriage was a mistake" is not enough. All the husband has to do to preserve the status quo is avoid taking action, asking for delays, failing to show up in court, and otherwise stonewalling and dragging things out in an attempt to wear her down. He doesn't want to grant her that wish.

My friend Tamar Denninberg lives in Jerusalem. She was a vibrant and bright young woman when she got married and then had a beautiful daughter. After only four years of marriage, she filed for divorce and has been fighting for it her entire youth. Her daughter is now 36, and she is now a 61-year-old woman who has lost all her joys, dreams, and hopes. She never dated another man and never had an opportunity to build a relationship. She has given up on starting a family.

Under Israeli law, she remains trapped in a defunct marriage that her husband won't allow to end or terminate. She can't legally remarry and was obligated even to repay some of his debts. "How come a woman's freedom is at the mercy of her husband?" she asks. "That law was written, maybe 4,000 years ago, but it put the woman in a place that she became invisible and helpless, and most of the time, completely dependent on her husband's will."

We are just two living examples of hundreds, perhaps thousands, of Israeli women caught in the legal and social limbo because of a law that leaves the matter of divorce for all Jewish citizens in the hands of a government-funded religious court. In Israel, there is neither civil marriage nor civil divorce; only rabbis can legalize a marriage or its dissolution, which is only possible with the husband's full consent.

If a woman has children with another man before a divorce is granted, those children and their descendants will be deemed illegitimate and not be allowed to marry in Israel under the current law. A Jewish man also needs his wife's permission to divorce; but without it, he can live with another woman and have children, who will be recognized as Jewish in Israel, while she cannot. The court, consisting of a panel of rabbis, bases its decisions on the customs of Orthodox Judaism. The rulings apply to all Jewish Israelis, whether Orthodox, Conservative or Reform, observant or secular. Around 35% of Jewish marriages in Israel end in divorce.

Letter from India

My name is Shayara Bano, I am 35, live in the Indian state of Uttar Pradesh, and have been married for 13 years. Last year I received an unusual letter from my husband, accusing me of stealing jewelry and money. He closed the letter with a single sentence, repeated three times: "I divorce you. I divorce you. I divorce you." He has not allowed me to even see my two children. I am among the countless Muslim women in India who have been abandoned by their husbands, often without any notice, through "triple talaq" permitted under Muslim family law that allows a Muslim man to instantaneously divorce his wife. After the grieving was over, I stood up and said "enough is enough" and filed a lawsuit against my husband in the Indian Supreme Court.

My friend Ishrat Jahan was only 14 when she became a bride. She and her husband were married for 15 years and had four children. In 2015, she was unceremoniously divorced over the phone. Her husband called her from Dubai, repeated "I divorce you" three times, and hung up. Ishrat is not even allowed to see her children. Along with other women, she is now also approaching the Supreme Court. "I want my children, I want alimony, and I want my home that my parents paid for."

The Quran's teachings on triple talaq require months of reconciliation attempts before the marriage can be dissolved. But our religious leaders don't adhere to that guidance. Many of India's Muslim clerics insist that the Indian judiciary has no right to interpret their religious texts. The All India Muslim Personal Law Board, a powerful organization that dictates family law, filed a 69-page affidavit in September countering Bano's case. "Male is (the) stronger and female weaker sex. Man is not dependent on (a) woman for his protection. On the contrary, she needs him for her defence (defense)," stated the affidavit, adding that triple talaq wards off the possibility of a rise in murders of women whose husbands want to divorce them.

India is the home to the world's third-largest Muslim population, with 90 million Muslim women. Roughly 10% are survivors of triple talaq, and the clear majority receive no compensation. In a 1985 landmark judgment, the Supreme Court granted divorcee, Shah Bano, alimony for life. But following protests from Muslim leaders and others that the court was being intrusive, the judgment was overturned.

Concluding Note:

For Divorce in Israel, please watch the movie GETT which is available on the internet. For Divorce in India, in August 2017, the Indian Supreme Court deemed instant triple talaq to be unconstitutional.

My Journey With Khizr

I have been patiently waiting for over ten years to get enough understanding before I opt to write this article. Allah (God) has provided me the guidance, and I humbly request Him to accept my work and forgive me for any unintentional error. This article deals with the journey of Moses (pbuh) with Khizr (as). Please recite Ayat 60 to Ayat 82 of the 18th Surah Al-Kahef in the Holy Quran, shown at the end of this article. Read its Translation and study its Tafseer. I had the burning question in my mind as to why Khizr killed the innocent boy. The answer that Khizr acted per Allah's command, or the boy would become a wicked son for his pious parents, failed to justify this example. I studied several writings and discussed the issue with many scholars. This article is my attempt to explore this issue. Insha Allah, my Lord will help me.

We are human beings and have two spans of life, one is our present life on this planet, and the other is our permanent life after death. I will focus only on the life we are all experiencing on earth and the world around us. Religion and science have provided us with limited knowledge about this world. We base our experience on the ability to see, smell, hear, taste, and touch the components of this planet. We justify our actions based on this limited knowledge and our evolving experience. This is the "seen world." There exists another parallel world, very close but not visible to us and not accessible by us. It is called the "unseen world" (Alam-e-Ghaib). Illustrations of this unseen world are the angels, Soul (rooh), Divine Revelations (wahi), life after death, heaven, hell, and other examples. There is an invisible curtain between the two worlds that will be raised on the day of judgment.

The purpose of human beings is to live on this earth in order to participate in the training that prepares us for the next life and the trials that qualify us for it. At the same time, the duties of the angels (and other such creations of Allah) involve managing the affairs of both the seen and unseen worlds according to Allah's orders. He has assigned these creations as the bureaucratic force for the management and administration of our seen world. These creations are living among us and are working continuously to manage this world, from significant tasks to essential details. They get their coursework and their orders from God. Some of them are given highly elevated assignments as prominent as the teaching of a Prophet. Khizr is one such example.

Khizr was assigned to educate Prophet Moses (pbuh) about the co-existence and inter-relationship between the seen and unseen worlds. He carefully selected three elementary and straightforward examples to elaborate on the difference between our knowledge about the seen world and the lack of knowledge about the unseen world. Something that may seem to us as completely unacceptable and totally unjustified may very well be within the norms of the unseen world.

Every day around us, we see a lot of incidents beyond the bounds of our intelligence, beyond the limits of our tolerance, and beyond the boundaries of our comprehension. Let me mention just one such example. Within a few seconds, over 100,000 humans died in the 2005 Kashmir earthquake in Pakistan. Over 138,000 were injured, and more than 3.5 million became homeless. Nineteen thousand innocent children were buried alive when their school buildings collapsed. How and why has this happened?

The life of a human being is sometimes beset by trials, tragedies, or calamities that appear to make no sense. Our human mind is incapable to comprehend these heartbreaking catastrophes. Most of us often ignore the existence of the unseen world. It is where the matters of our seen world are decided. These bureaucratic forces do administer the Divine planning and implement the Divine policies. Upon finalizing His decisions, Allah issues orders to these forces for execution. Therefore, no matter what we decide on this earth, it needs the blessing of Allah. The knowledge Allah teaches His servants is of two types, knowledge that is acquired through human effort and knowledge that Allah teaches from Himself. Allah describes Khizr as, "One whom I taught knowledge from Myself."

Khizr killed the innocent boy only as a metaphorical illustration to show Moses that his action may not be allowed under the laws of this seen world and is unacceptable for our civilization. It was conducted for a very specific reason, for the benefit of humans, and with the authorization of our Lord. Khizr carefully selected a very controversial and provocative scenario to demonstrate his teaching. The act that Khizr did was purely from Allah's destiny. He made it take place in Khizr's hands so that the believers could use it as a stunning example of the subtle benefits of what Allah has destined. It was not conducted as a random act of violence or a shallow action of cruelty. It was handled with thorough analysis and considering the results and impacts of this action for both the present and the future of the humans involved.

For a brief duration of time, Khizr lifted the curtain between the seen and unseen worlds and let Moses observe the strategies and procedures of the unseen world.

We should have full faith in the wisdom of what is happening in the Divine Factory. If the veil were removed from the "unseen", we would come to know that what is taking place here is for the best. Khizr was telling Moses to have complete faith in the mercy of our Lord and not give up hope when things around us go beyond the comprehension of our human brain. There are paradoxes in life where apparent loss is, in fact, a gain, and what appears to be cruelty is, in fact, mercy. Khizr repeatedly told Moses to have patience. Let us learn from Moses that patience is often a virtue. This story is about a good outcome from a horrible situation. The lesson for us humans is never to be frustrated if something terrible happens to you. Allah will bring you a good result and reward you for your patience. Bad things can happen to good people, but do not be disappointed because our knowledge is limited only to our seen world. The results we consider as lousy today may turn out to have a positive impact on our lives later. Face your problems with hope and trust in a fair and merciful Allah. He is there for us and will help us overcome our problems. Our Lord is the most merciful, most beneficial. I wonder now who is the wise Khizr that is walking beside me on my present journey.

English Translation of the text of
Verses 60 to 82 of Chapter 18 Al-Kahf (The Cave)
of the Holy Quran

(And recount to them the story of Moses) when Moses said to his servant: "I will journey on until I reach the point where the two rivers meet, though I may march on for ages." But when they reached the point where the two rivers meet, they forgot their fish, and it took its way into the sea, as if through a tunnel. When they had journeyed further on, Moses said to his servant: "Bring us our repast. We are surely fatigued by today's journey." The servant said: "Did you see what happened? When we betook ourselves to the rock to take rest, I forgot the fish, and it is only Satan who caused me to forget to mention it to you so that it made its way into the sea in a strange manner." Moses said: "That is what we were looking for." So the two turned back, retracing their footsteps.

And there they found one of Our servants upon whom We had bestowed Our mercy, and to whom We had imparted a special knowledge from Ourselves. Moses said to him: "May l follow you that you may teach me something of the wisdom which you have been taught?" He answered: "You will surely not be able to bear with me. For how can you patiently bear with something you cannot encompass in your knowledge?" Moses replied: "You shall find me, if Allah wills, patient; and I shall not disobey you in anything." He said: "Well if you follow me, do not ask me concerning anything until I mention it to you."

Then the two went forth until, when they embarked on the boat, he made a hole in it, at which point Moses exclaimed: "Have you made a hole in it to drown the people in the boat? You have certainly done an awful thing." He replied: "Did I not tell you that you will not be able to bear with me patiently?" Moses said: "Do not take me to the task at my forgetfulness, and do not be hard on me." Then the two went forth until they met a lad whom he slew, at which point Moses exclaimed: "What! Have you slain an innocent person without his having slain anyone? Surely you have done a horrible thing." He said: "Did I not tell you that you will not be able to bear with me patiently?" Moses said: "Keep me no more in your company if I question you concerning anything after this. You will then be fully justified." Then the two went forth until they came to a town, they asked its people for food, but they refused to play host to them. They found in that town a wall that was on the verge of tumbling down, and he bolstered it, whereupon Moses said: "If you had wished, you could have received payment for it." He said: "This brings me and you to a parting of ways. Now I shall explain the true meaning of things about which you could not remain patient.

As for the boat, it belonged to some poor people who worked on the river, and I desired to damage it, for beyond them lay the dominion of a king who was wont to seize every boat by force. As for the lad, his parents were people of faith, and we feared lest he should plague them with transgression and disbelief., and we desired that their Lord should grant them another in his place, a son more upright and more tender-hearted. As for the wall, it belonged to two orphan boys in the city, and under it, there was a treasure that belonged to them. Their father was a righteous man, and your Lord intended that they should come of age and then bring forth their treasure as a mercy from your Lord; I did not do this of my own bidding. This is the true meaning of things with which you could not keep your patience."

The Elite Muslim

This article is written as a satire and exaggerates
the realities on the ground.

Please read it with a grain of salt.

L ast week some of our old "friends" got together for
lunch at a local desi restaurant. Someone suggested that
we should celebrate our 50 years of accomplishments in
South Florida. Celebrate? Accomplishments?? What in the
world are we talking about??? Of course, we have built some
masjids. These buildings sit empty for most of the week besides Friday congregation and Sunday school. Christians,
Jews, Hindus, and other faiths have built far better institutions, which are places of family gathering, social interaction,
youth participation, community assistance, emergency help,
and worship.

Let me describe the portrait of an apparently true Muslim, which is on display in our masjids. We can call this class

the Elite Muslim. The Elites have their own established groups, and they do not want to pollute their faith by mixing with the non-elites. There is hope. You can join them and become an Elite if you fulfill these requirements.

- The male Elite is prohibited from growing a mustache on his face.

- He must grow a beard and let it grow to unlimited reach. He is not supposed to touch it, trim it, wash it or comb it. He becomes a sign of horror for a small child in a dark alley.

- He cannot complete a single sentence without saying Insha-Allah (God Willing).

- A male Muslim is not worthy of joining the Elite class if he offers Salats at home.

- He is encouraged to be dressed in a long dress used by Arabs and a round cap on the head. No jeans or T-shirts, please. He will get extra points if he carries a red or blue Palestinian-style checkered scarf on his shoulder.

- He needs to replace Ramzan with Ramadan, Zuhr with Duhar, and Hadees with Hadiths.

- Prefer to quote Hadees and the sayings of the religious icons. If you don't mention the Quran, it's ok.

- Consider Birthdays, Valentine's, and Halloween as Haram.

- Recite and memorize the Quran in Arabic, and not necessarily read its translation, and understand it.

- And the most important requirement to be an Elite Muslim is that he must become a selfish person. He should care about his prayers, his rewards, and his place in Heaven. He doesn't have to care about others. Emphasis on Huqooqul Allah, and not on Huqooqul Ibad.

- He uses the inventions of non-Muslims, in his daily life, 24/7, but always calls them bad names. They represent the devil and will all go to Hell.

- He is always in a serious posture and does not dare to smile.

- The female Elites must wear a Niqab or at least a Hijab, and cover themselves from head to toe. They have to offer their Salats behind the males, behind opaque curtains.

Now I want to examine myself. What have I accomplished during the past 50 years in South Florida? The answer is zero. I have accomplished nothing that I can stand up proudly and mention. Indeed, I raised three beautiful children, and now I have eight adorable grandchildren. However, I will praise my wife for their upbringing, education, and marriage. I have bank accounts and properties. Again, the credit goes to my wife. What have I accomplished to show you?

I always played by the book. From the age of 10, I was always pushed to study harder and harder. I was told that I needed a top-notch education to find an excellent job, a good-looking wife, and a lovely house and car. So, I worked hard. I did not enjoy my youth or my midlife. I got into the Engineering College by depriving myself of any extracurricular activities. I had no life. I became book smart, but I was never street smart. Throughout my career, I was a door mat. Everyone walked all over me. I tried to take refuge in the religion, but I was disappointed when I tried to follow the Elites.

During these 50 years, I have developed some friendships. However, they are friends for the good times. Just getting together at a restaurant and filling ourselves with food that our wives won't allow us at home. Most of these friends live within a 25-mile radius but never care to call me for weeks. When I try to reach them, they do not pick up the phone. One day I saw a missed call on my phone from a dear friend. I immediately called him back. He told me that he had connected my number by mistake. He was trying to reach someone else.

In case of emergency, I wonder if I will be able to contact any of my friends. Recently, during an emergency, I tried to reach several friends. I had to leave messages, and they returned my call days after the crisis was over. Except for one person. He came running to help me and gave me the key to his house. I stayed at his home for more than a week and freeloaded on his food. My dear friend, thank you from the bottom of my heart. God bless you and reward you. A friend in need is a friend indeed.

I am still not convinced about the idea of a celebration for us being here for 50 years. Our celebration involves boring speeches and food. We discuss only two topics, politics, and religion. Nobody talks about literature, art, TV, movies, social media, innovation, or intelligence. You don't laugh and dare not tell a joke unless it is an Islamic joke. Islamic joke???

On top of all this, South Florida has become the Mecca for fundraising. We invite speakers from out of state or even out of the country, pay for the speech, travel, and accommodation. I remember when a local masjid invited the sister of the British PM, who had converted to Islam. She requested that, in addition, we should bear the cost of her family to travel to Disney World, including tickets and accommodation. I don't want to be part of such a celebration. Thank you, my friend.

Why Do We Want
To Get Married?

Several decades ago, during my college years, I pretended to be a palm reader. Believe me; I have no clue about palmistry. I got popular and was able to hold some gorgeous hands. Almost all the girls wanted to know about their wedding. When are they going to get married and to whom? Girls start dreaming about marriage as soon as they hit the teens, maybe earlier. They do all their planning for the few days of the dream wedding and hardly think about the many years of real married life that follows. They live in the imaginary Cinderella castle and dream about the prince charming who will sweep them away. Boys, on the other hand, are just plain stupid. A thirteen-year-old boy has no idea what we are talking about. And of course, the parents are a generation behind.

Companionship

It is hard to be a good spouse unless you know the needs and wishes of your partner. Companionship is the paramount outcome of married life. Our journey on this earth is full of ups and downs, and you need a partner to go through this challenging passage. If you are unwilling to be a full-time companion and a lifetime partner to your spouse, you should think seriously before tying the knots. In addition to the obvious need for companionship, I came up with three Ss for boys, Sex, Service, and Support, and three Ps for girls, Provider, Protector, and Pursue of Happiness.

The Three Ss

I will come out and say it bluntly that sex is on top of the list for boys. Therefore girls, please pay attention. This is a family forum, and therefore I will stop here. Although Muslim countries have record population explosions, we dare not say a word about this taboo on a public platform.

The next S is Service. The man looks for a home that he can come to at the end of the day. I am not talking about the house being his castle or other such nonsense. But he needs someone to be there, eat dinner with him, spend time together, discuss family issues and enjoy playing with the kids.

The last and vital need of a man is his wife's support. You know that behind every successful man, there is a woman. We are talking about the support provided by his wife. Please support him in going through the difficulties and encourage him to deal with life. Support does not mean saying yes sir. If he wants to start a new project, get involved and advise him about the pitfalls if you feel so. If he makes a mistake, try to help him, don't blame him, and don't criticize him. Encourage him to pick up the pieces and move forward. A wife's support is a must for the progress of her husband.

The Three Ps

The girl is looking for a husband who will be the main bread earner for the family, even though both may be bringing in the money. She is looking for a responsible and dependable person who will provide for the family, for their necessities of living, even though she may be getting a higher salary. This is an important issue; however, her parents place too much emphasis on this and not on the other two Ps.

The next quality of a good husband is to look after his wife and children during both the good times and challenging periods. She needs to feel safe and protected. The guy must provide shelter that she can call her home and a place to raise their children. He needs to protect her from the mischiefs of life as much as he can. And even if you cannot, guys just show off, pretend to be Salman Khan. Believe me, it works most of the time.

The third P is for the pursuit of happiness. Out of all the qualities and requirements of a good husband, this stands out to be the most important for the girl. The main reason a girl wants to marry is to pursue happiness in life. She wants a partner that will give her joy. And guys, this is not easy. Men have very little understanding of how to make her happy. Therefore, boys need to do a lot of homework. I would have given you some points, but this is where I have failed miserably in my own marriage. May God have mercy on me. This P includes everything that she wants in his personality, tall, handsome, and who will make her laugh.

The Balloons

I want to leave with one piece of advice to all the girls and boys who are thinking of getting married. Please look beyond the wedding day. Discuss the basics of married life with your parents or other married family members and friends close to you. Try to get a good read on this subject. And if you are already married but are not happy with your spouse, please do this. There is a 2007 Indian movie Dus Kahaniyan, which has ten short stories. One of these stories is titled "Ghubbare," which means balloons. It may be only ten minutes long and is available on YouTube. It will guide you to understanding the secret of a happy partnership.

Verse 187 of Chapter 2 of the Quran states: "They are your garments, and you are their garments." This Ayat is the most beautiful metaphor expressing the relationship between a husband and his wife. Remember that marriage is a very sacred and noble step in your life. Please respect it, enjoy its pleasures and cherish its values. Happy Valentine.

Tolerance

A Muslim's perspective on
Life in the United States

L ast summer, we visited the beautiful Fort Lauderdale Beach with our guests. Both families with small children and grandchildren enjoyed a sunny Florida afternoon. The children were playing in the sand, the men went into the water, and the ladies enjoyed the breeze and socializing with each other. Next to our bench was an Arab family with their children. The father took the kids into the ocean. The children were splashing in the water and enjoying the surf. The family was having fun.

I saw the mother, an attractive woman, dressed in a black abaya covering her from head to toe, except for her face. She sat on the bench and watched her family enjoying the beach. Less than 100 feet from her was an American woman lying on the sand in a short two-piece bikini that barely covered her privates. She was quietly sunbathing on her beach towel. These two women tolerated each other. They tolerated their attires, outfits, and appearances.

The Arab woman did not criticize the American woman for not properly covering up her body, and the American woman did not criticize the Arab woman for covering up her body too much at the beach. They tolerated their presence within 100 feet of each other with such a vast difference in dress code and morality. This is the beauty of America. The Arab woman then offered the Asar Salat while sitting on the bench. The American woman got up, looked at the Arab women, and smiled and waved. The Arab woman smiled and nodded. They both accepted each other's existence at that location, and both were able to enjoy the beach.

I can tell you many such examples of tolerance in non-Muslim countries. I wrote a long paragraph about "tolerance" in Muslim countries, which I deleted. Tolerance means accepting and valuing differences between people. It is a moral obligation that involves mutual respect and consideration between people. Tolerance is the virtue of a civilized age, whereas intolerance is the sign of an inadequate education system. Last summer, Pope Francis said in an interview, "If someone is gay and searching for the Lord and has goodwill, then who am I to judge him?"

Despite its many flaws and problems, America is a beautiful country with virtues such as tolerance, freedoms, social justice, and many other values. I will attempt to write more about them. I love America. This is the home of my children, grandchildren, and their children.

A Life Wasted

After 78 years on this planet, every new morning is getting me closer to my final destination, when I will be facing my Creator. Allah (God) will ask me, Oh my servant, I have granted you a long life, given you time, wealth, dignity, and intelligence. I have blessed you with good health, decent education, loving and caring parents, and obedient children. I have given you a life that millions of other humans dream of. What have you done with this life? What are your accomplishments? In front of my Creator, on that day, I will be standing with empty hands, my head down and my face deep in embarrassment. I have nothing to show except for three well-raised children, and even that credit goes to my spouse.

Our beloved prophet (pbuh) received the first verse of the Quran at the age of 40 and passed away from this world when he was 63. In these 23 years (20 solar years), he revolutionized the world. The first 13 years in Mecca were full of struggles, and only during the short period of the last ten years in Medina did he establish Allah's religion and His sovereignty. Not in books and speeches, but in reality, in the everyday practical lives of ordinary people on this earth. I cannot compare myself to our beloved Prophet (pbuh), but I have his clear example to follow. I have been in the United States for over 50 years and have achieved nothing for my religion, my country, or even my community.

There are millions of more qualified engineers and more intelligent human beings than I. However, Allah selected me to go to the United States and granted me a high-level engineering career, a dignified status, prosperity, and wisdom. I was given all the time, resources, and position to do good for my fellow humans. However, I always placed my own interest above other noble deeds. I acquired property, bank accounts, nice cars, and other materialistic goals. To suppress my guilt, I gave a little handout and some leftovers to a few charities.

So, on the day when I face my Creator, with empty hands and my head down in embarrassment, I will reply to my Lord, my Rab: "Oh Allah, You gave me everything except one. I have no courage. I am a coward person, and I was never able to stand up for myself or my goals. I always compromised and said yes-sir. I always accepted the results and never tried to defeat others for my own advantage. With all Your blessings and gifts, I remained a no-name, dull, below-average ordinary human being. Yes, my Lord, I have not fulfilled my duties. A lifetime without any accomplishment is a life wasted. Yes, my Lord, I have wasted this precious life that You have granted me on this earth, and I have returned to face You with empty hands."

The end is near, and I can feel the finish line. Today I am very frustrated, feeling suffocated, and depressed to the point that I no longer believe in Duaa (supplication). However, I raise these empty hands for maybe the last time. "Oh my Lord, my Rab, Oh Allah, please give me a peaceful death with Eman. Please grant me forgiveness. You are Rehman and Raheem (Most Gracious and Most Merciful). Aameen."

Made in the USA
Columbia, SC
17 November 2022

71495875R00075